DEEP
GROOVES

DEEP
GROOVES

Overcoming Patterns
That Keep You Stuck

LISA LINFIELD

ISBN: 978-0-620-87673-5
Ebook ISBN: 978-0-620-88354-2

www.LisaLinfield.com/DeepGrooves

The purpose of Deep Grooves: Overcoming Patterns That Keep You Stuck is to provide the reader with insight in the hope that it will shift their thinking patterns. It is sold with the understanding that it is not intended to provide individualised advice specific to each unique reader.

While the publisher and author have made every attempt to verify that the information provided in this book is correct and up to date, the publisher and author assume no responsibility for any error, inaccuracy, or omission. The advice, examples, and strategies contained in this book are not suitable for every person or situation, and results are not guaranteed.

Cover designed by Lisa Barbee
Illustrations by Sonja Niederhumer
Typeset by Kaitlin Barwick

This book is dedicated to my family.

With them, I belong. With their love and support,
they give me the strength to believe I can do anything,
to strive to be a better version of myself.

John, Jess, Isi, and Em—I love you with all my heart and am so
grateful to be surrounded by your love and laughter daily.

Mum, Dad, and Nick—my first family—the love and support you
gave and continue to give are the roots that anchor my tree.

Contents

My Gift to You ix

Introduction 1

Why "the Truth" Is Not the Truth

1: Why "the Truth" Is Not the Truth 8

2: Removing the Weeds That Strangle Our Best Life Tree 13

3: The World Out There Tells You Such Crap 25

4: Short-Term Hits of Happiness 33

5: Assumptions Become Our Identity 43

6: Fitting In Versus Belonging 56

7: The Groove 73

8: The Gap 82

Signposts to Your Best Life

9: Listening to Your Gut: The Guiding Signposts 94

10: Understanding the Signposts That Have Been 103

11: Understanding the Signposts That Are Now 115

12: Looking from the Outside In 123

13: Permission to Dream 134

Little-Known Secrets for Step-Change Success

14: Free Your Mind for the Best Chance of Success 146

15: Rocket Fuel 156

Contents

16: Shortcuts to Power 165

17: The Force Is Strong, So Be Prepared 174

18: Getting Stuff Done: The Practices That
    Nurture Your Best Life Tree 184

19: Transitioning 196

Call to Action 200

Notes 201

About the Author 204

My Gift to You

This book is for all of us who feel the built-in desire to grow as a human. To be the best version of ourselves we can be.

Yet for most of us, each day feels similar to the next, despite the whisper of our hearts that we were made for so much more. The gnawing feeling every now and then that there's a gap between who we are and the potential we have innately within us.

For some of us, that gap is the work we do, our career or business. For others, it's the health you know you need. It could be relationships or financial freedom.

Whether it's our inner fears, the storms we've weathered through life, or that we are so far stuck in our groove we can't see another way, we find ourselves going through the motions in parts of our life. "It's just the way it is," we tell ourselves. But somewhere deep in us we sense that we were made for more, and our soul prods us, "Is this all there is to life?" as it tries to highlight the gap between our unique purpose and the Deep Groove we're stuck in.

The real, lasting change needed to shift anything in our lives—not the quick-fix, filtered social media type of change—starts with shifting the way we think about things. But the challenge is our brains are wired not to embrace the change that takes us from our comfort zone. Our brains are wired to keep us safe, within the tribe, within the way The World Out There has said life should be.

But you were created uniquely—strengths and weaknesses—for your journey in life. Not The World Out There's prescription of what you should do and what should make you happy, yours. And now's the time to rise up, be brave, and climb out of the groove of comfort.

This book will help you understand that journey. It's practical, deeply personal, and my hope is that it will start highlighting the signposts for your Best Life.

In addition, making the changes we need to make always has three practical pieces to it:

1. Find a teacher to learn from.
2. Get accountability partners.
3. Surround yourself with people who are journeying on your path to support you.

So I've created a safe place where you can learn from like-minded people who are also on this journey to live their "Best Life." You will learn deeply from their experiences, be encouraged by their progress and can find an accountability partner to walk this journey with you. You'll also find me there to cheer you on, and together with my team, we can answer your questions. For the brief moments you're with us each day, you can feel like you're walking in a groove of like-minded humans, cheering for your success. It's a Facebook Group you can find at www.facebook.com/groups/BraveToBeFree or you can find a link to it by going to www.LisaLinfield.com/DeepGrooves.

Besides community, many of you have asked where you can learn more. Because our brains don't work the same and we all learn differently, I try as hard as possible to create supporting content in different thinking styles.

Some people are conceptual and want to learn more about the ideas in the book, whilst others are doers and want more information on the 'How To.' Some love to know the 'Behind the Scenes.' But the science shows that all of us will gain 42 percent more impact if we write down what we're learning. So there are worksheets, blog articles, behind the scenes, interactive questionnaires, and other tools to help you step change to reach your Best Life. Visit www.LisaLinfield.com /DeepGrooves and get what you need to go deeper into this journey.

Then every week on a Wednesday, I release a new episode on my podcast *Working Women's Wealth*. I alternate the weeks between an interview with an amazing woman, and a short 10–20 minute teaching on mindset, wealth, work, happiness, change, or generally living your Best Life. So subscribe via your favourite podcast app, download it when you're on Wi-Fi, and listen to it when you commute to work or exercise so you can continue to push yourself to make the changes you need.

Lastly, there are three places you can find me: My Instagram account is @LisaLinfieldPage which has similar content to my Facebook page @LisaLinfieldPage. For those with an interest in money, my Facebook Page @WorkingWomensWealth is where I focus on my goal to teach a million women about money.

Introduction

What if everything you've ever believed as truth your whole life is *not* right—or maybe not totally right?

Each of us makes big and small decisions every single day, based on the knowledge we have at the time.

These decisions are a combination of factual knowledge; circumstances; the way we've been brought up to think; what "The World Out There" and the latest news cycle tells us; and for some, what our gut tells us. Sometimes we are on autopilot—doing things one way because that's the way it's always been done—and sometimes we cannot see a clear way forward, so we just pin the tail on the donkey, hoping it's in the right spot. Over time our actions become habits, the way we are in relationships becomes set, and our thinking goes to autopilot—all forming grooves in our life that sometimes become so deep we can't see out of the canyon, and we conclude that this is the way it's always going to be.

But what if we're wrong?

Our brains have evolved over many, many years with one primary function: to protect the species and keep it safe, to make sure there's a next generation to ensure our survival. The brain's design is awe-inspiring, and its ability to process at a speed of eleven million bits of information per second fills me with great respect for it. Our brains decipher all those signals, then file and tag them deep in our subconscious to develop shortcuts for quicker retrieval and processing as well as to save energy.

But everything in life has a light side and a shadow side. The brain's primary function of safety means that we're wired *not* to step outside our comfort zone. As the saying goes, "A ship in harbor is safe, but that is not what ships are built for."[1] Similarly, the brain's shortcuts used for great speed and energy efficiency can also lead to the shadow side of bad habits and faulty assumptions. This means there are flaws in your thinking, and it's possible that the decisions you've made in the past or the things you've chosen to do were in fact chosen based on incorrect or faulty logic.

Growing Up: Science = Fact = Truth

In school during my growing-up years and in my first undergraduate study at medical school, logic and reasoning were always so highly prized. Maths and science were king, and medicine was all about *proven* clinical trials—and the results of those trials were considered conclusive, facts. There was a right way and a wrong way, and anything non-scientific was dismissed.

So you can imagine how life in the real world smacked me!

In my first job after university, I had two patients with very similar whiplash injuries. Both had been injured in the same kind of car accident—they were waiting to turn and got hit by someone shooting a traffic light. The big difference was that one woman lost her two-year-old child in the accident, and the other was by herself in the car. I remember clearly how the woman who lost her child just struggled to get better. In contrast, the one who was alone in the car took just six weeks to be pain-free.

Now I know that medically there are a million other factors that could have come into play in their results. But the symptoms and treatments were so similar and the outcomes so dramatically different. Looking at the differences in these two cases, I noticed for the first time that the science and medical worldview I was taught was not the whole picture. That maybe, just maybe, there was a gap in the completeness of the "clinical trial evidence"—the human, emotional, non-"scientific" variables too complex to be isolated, quantified, and tested in a university laboratory. How do you ethically test the impact of losing a child on the rate of healing when compared to someone who didn't suffer that loss?

The medical body of knowledge took fifty years to double in 1950. Just thirty years later, in 1980, it took seven years to double. If you started medical school in 2010, by the time you had finished the minimum seven-year training, the body of knowledge would have doubled three times. And it's estimated that in 2020 it will take just seventy-three days.[2]

What us medical school students in the 1990s thought was fact and the whole picture was nowhere near that—both because so much had yet to be discovered and because so much couldn't be distilled by a lab. Yet inside the groove of the canyon of our minds, we believed that this was *the* reality, the only way forward, the whole truth.

As each of us has journeyed through life, let's be honest—it's given us a few smacks the fairy tales never told us about. What I realise with each setback is that what I took as black or white, as truth and logic, has many more shades of grey than I'd ever considered.

Quality Doing Needs Quality Thinking

Nancy Kline says, "The quality of everything human beings do . . . depends on the quality of the thinking we do first."[3]

The challenge is that as we keep going at life's hectic pace, we very seldom stop to ask ourselves, "Why do I believe what I believe? And is it the whole truth??" We live life stuck in our grooves, believing with all our hearts the "Good Reasons" for behaving the way we do, never taking the time to delve into the "Real Reasons" for our behaviour and decisions.

It all boils down to the fact that for everything we say and do, there's a deep pattern of thinking—both subconsciously and consciously—that comes before it. Stuff that's been synthesised and codified into our brain in such a way that we don't have to think about *why* we think it, we just do—a shortcut to save energy. If we each want to live our Best Life, we need to make sure that we have our best understanding of what we think and why we think the thoughts we do so we can understand our behaviour and change it if we need to.

When I left the corporate world after twenty years, I thought the hardest thing about setting up my wealth management business would be building a customer base and brand and keeping up to date with the global and local economies. That was hard, but not even close to how intense the personal journey has been for me.

This personal journey involved discovering that what I thought was the whole world (from my viewpoint deep inside the groove of the corporate canyon) was in fact a small groove of a riverbed. And who I was after twenty years in that corporate machine was just a reflection in the stream, distorted by the corporate tribe. Keeping up with the global economy had nothing on my struggle to overcome fears I didn't even know I had. I had to rediscover my voice, opinions, and perspectives that had long been dulled as I adapted to fit in. I struggled to find strength and confidence within myself as I realised that my whole life my self-esteem had come from parents, teachers, professors, and then bosses who all told me what a good little girl I was. The reflection in the stream of Lisa as the over-achiever was such a one-sided distortion of who I was as a holistic human.

I'm learning that if I want to be truly free, I'm only one brave step away at any moment in time. I can choose to do the safe thing . . . or I can choose to be brave. But I'm also learning that I can't do either if I don't force myself to take the time to reflect, to question my assumptions, to differentiate between Good Reasons and Real Reasons, to be brutally honest, and to challenge myself to be mindful. Every day, I must choose *my* path, *my* groove—not just the easy one or familiar one I've been in for so long because it's easier than climbing out the canyon.

Our Unique Purpose

I believe deeply that each of us was born a completely unique human, with unique talents and flaws in a combination that's designed specifically for our purpose in life. It's not random that you are who you are. For some of us, that purpose is to raise two phenomenal humans; for others, it's to change the world's perception of climate change, or to love and nurture people in the last days of their life, or to be the ultimate mom to your fur baby.

Whatever that purpose is, *both* our flaws *and* our gifts were specifically combined to enable us to live our best lives. But here's the catch. Our greatness is not found in the comfort of life. In fact, the comfort of life shrinks our greatness. It's found just outside, by pushing those boundaries that keep us safe. Saying those things that we shy away from. Ignoring everything The World Out There tells us will make us happy and finding our unique answer to the question of happiness. Greatness demands that we struggle to identify and then use the gifts we were given to serve the greater good.

Each of us has our own Best Life we are to lead. Yours may be alone in the mountains or in the slums in India or in the centre of New York. Discovering and living your Best Life *is* the quest, a quest made so much harder by the fact that our brains are bombarded by The World Out There with opinions of who we are, who we're meant to be, and what will make us happy every minute of every day of every year from the moment we're born.

But what if all those messages your brain received, everything that makes up your identity and belief system, the basis of every decision (and therefore action) are all wrong for you . . . and you've never taken the time to think about it?

Why "the Truth" Is Not the Truth

1

Why "the Truth"
Is Not the Truth

I was three or four years old when I struck gold. My dad had been on a business trip to America and had come back with some "koki" marker pens. We never had these in South Africa—or at least no one I knew at play school or our family friends had anything nearly as cool as this.

These pieces of gold were in the shape of a triangular mouse, with a bright-coloured round butt narrowing into a lid with a little white face complete with whiskers and ears. Not only were they cute, but the colours were amazing and not as smudgy as a traditional crayon or chalk.

I was beside myself with excitement, knowing I was going to be *the* coolest kid at play school the next day. That morning I was up, dressed, and ready to go *way* earlier than I needed to be, brimming with excitement. Needless to say, the teachers and my friends were all very impressed with this new addition, so at break time I had an idea.

In the playground was an old car that sat on its belly, grass growing within the tyre-less wheel cavities. I sat on the front of it and made each child line up as I proceeded to draw on their faces. I was the chief, and they were all part of my tribe. When I'd finished decorating their faces and had one of them decorate mine, I jumped on the front of the car, looked down at them all, raised my arms high in the air in triumphant victory, and said some stirring speech. Jumping off the car, we burst into fun play, celebrating the occasion.

The bell rang, and laughing and full of energy, we returned to the class at the end of break. Initially, the teachers joined in with our energy and enthusiasm, and then instructed us to all go wash our faces.

But that laughter quickly turned into panic when they realised they were unable to scrub the ink off our faces. The ink was permanent marker. I suddenly found myself in so much trouble, shouted at and sent to the corner of the room to wait out the rest of the day.

The fall from vivacious leader of this giggling tribe to outcast in a matter of minutes was massive. The shame was overwhelming for a three-year-old unable to fully comprehend why the sunshine had turned into a storm. Later, the shame was intensified by the horror of the children's parents and the scorn of my own as they learnt why I was being suspended from pre-school.

The teacher at play school may have been lovely, but the combination of her handling and my interpretation of the event through the eyes of a three-year-old had such a deep impact on my life. The lesson my little brain learnt was to never claim your space as leader, to stay in the background because it saved you from isolation, loneliness, shame, and rejection. It kept you safe.

As an adult, I look back at that experience and I want to jump into that scene and hold that scared little freckly redhead tight and tell her to *never* let other people's reactions stop her from jumping on the car and leading her tribe. I want to explain to her that adults like things neat and tidy, including their little poppets, and that sometimes they can overreact. They aren't trying to be mean, but in the heat of the moment, they just value order over life's precious lessons. Sometimes they don't think deeply about what they're saying, and their instinctive reaction is to return things back to the comfort of the way they were as quickly as possible.

But even now as I write this response to that little girl with the logic and perspective of the adult, I feel this crushing, burning feeling in the middle of my chest as the shame washes over me. It amazes me how the emotion of that three-year-old's memory can overpower a far better, more logical adult interpretation of the event.

Journeying with Jess

Becoming a parent has been one of the most humbling journeys I've ever been on. My three girls have very different strengths and challenges and, therefore, very different parenting needs. As Jess, my eldest, grows, I get to go back and re-think my experiences of childhood, as in many ways she is very similar to me. She is gentle, kind, and soft-hearted and struggles at school to navigate the meanness of girls—their flip-flopping in friendships or their fights that take others in the group as collateral damage—just as I did.

As she tells me her stories, it's like she's retelling my own experiences from thirty years earlier, so I am able to deeply empathise. Yet I have the logic of an adult now to see how faulty my interpretation was at the time and how those assumptions have negatively impacted my journey, stopping me from living my Best Life. I can see the other children's fickleness for what it is—hurtful words that they don't mean or that come from a place of their own deep hurt. Those nasty words are intended to elevate themselves in the group as each one jockeys to be accepted by the bully, who is often one of the most broken girls. Many times, these girls have tough home situations and are battling their own demons, looking to fill up their own love bucket with popularity and adoration from the girls and boys in their world.

How Our Thinking Stack Develops

Our thoughts over time become our worldview, the framework on which we base all our decisions. These layers of experiences stack sequentially on one another. But without intervention, each experience just layers on the other, with the lumps and bumps of hurtful experiences compacting down over time and forming grooves of behaviour we just slot into automatically, changing our path without us knowing. Like the famous tale of The Princess and The Pea, the pre-school experience becomes the pea in the layers of mattresses, invisible to The World Out There but causing such pain to the princess.

How Our Thinking Stack Develops

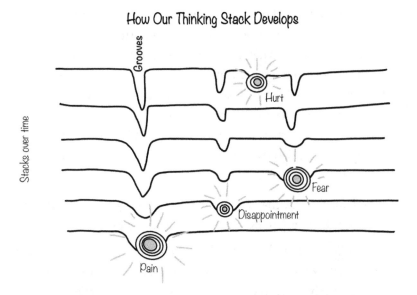

The problem is that as we get older and wiser and our brain develops more complicated processing capabilities, it doesn't automatically go back and re-process each event. Nor does it apply a weighting scale to reduce the importance of the three-year-old's interpretation as the thirty-year-old has new experiences. It simply lays down the latest event within the framework it's developed until that point, regardless of how immature it is.

Our deepest views of our self and our world are formed through the following "Thinking Stack" Framework:

1. We experience an **event**—something we did, saw, read, or witnessed around us that happened in The World Out There or to us and that generated certain emotions.

2. We **interpret** the meaning of that event—based on the age, stage, and brain's developmental capacity *at the time*. In addition, we take into consideration the interpretations of the others at the event—our teachers, friends, or parents. We then link that event to others of a similar nature in our past and join dots that may or may not be correct to create cause-and-effect links in order to understand the potential consequences and impact on our safety, security, or status.

3. We then form shortcut **assumptions** that the brain uses to tag and store that event so that at a later stage it can quickly access those shortcuts to warn us of potential harm or draw us to potential opportunity.

4. Only later will we be able to see how our brain stored that experience, interpretation, and assumptions as we either (i) think about a new situation and are mindful of our thinking process or (ii) actively reflect on a past event or (iii) act in the moment of a new context.

When we look at that framework, it's so easy to see how many opportunities there are to develop faulty thinking processes.

As a child we don't have the emotional skillset to correctly interpret the events we experience. Mean, hurtful children put us down to make themselves feel more powerful. Our interpretations of those events come from other kids too scared to intervene or tired adults just wanting the noise on the playground to disappear, and so our brain forms assumptions based on such flawed thinking. But to us that assumption becomes fact, the truth on which we base all other assumptions to come.

If "The quality of everything we do . . . depends on the quality of the thinking we do first" as Nancy Kline says, then the most important thing we can do is go back and relook at our Thinking Stacks. We can question how true all those messages are that we absorbed from The World Out There and accepted as fact so that the things we do, the life we lead, has a chance of being our Best Life and not one based on the thinking of a young child in a broken world.

2

Removing the Weeds That Strangle Our Best Life Tree

Our brain is a complex but archaic piece of machinery, phenomenal in its capabilities. Understanding how it works is key to the shortcuts to changing our brain. In its simplest interpretation, it is comprised of three layers:

1. The upper, "human" brain responsible for reason, judgement, planning, and self-control that also acts mostly at a conscious level;
2. A middle or "mammalian" brain that contains emotions and memory and operates at a subconscious level;
3. And lastly, a primitive "reptilian" brain that is responsible for survival, keeping us safe, alive, fed, watered, breathing, and reproducing—all subconsciously.

In the lower subconscious portion of the brain is a part the size of your baby fingertip called the amygdala. Its job is to integrate sensory information, emotional behaviour, and motivation. Many parts of our brain all provide input into this little almond-shaped hub, where it triggers the quickest response to what it perceives "out there." This is where fear lives, as well as our response to threat—fight, flight, or freeze.

The problem with our lower brain is that so much of its operating system was developed in the days of tribal living, when fitting into the tribe and avoiding lions and other threats ensured you stayed safe, didn't venture into territory "out there" that belonged to other tribes, and survived. Maslow's hierarchy of needs of protection and provision are governed right here.

When we mess up, our ancient brain fears that the tribe will kick us out. We want to fight to defend ourselves or flee to hide from the threat. All the voices from The World Out There yell in our ear to pull us back in line with their thinking. For example:

- You see, you should have listened to our definition of happiness.
- You should have stayed in the background.
- You shouldn't have ventured to the land that the Successful People own. You don't belong there.

The problem is our world now is very different from the world our amygdala grew up in. It correctly developed through evolution to keep us safe inside the tribe. But now, the world is different. We will not die if we step outside our home suburb or what The World Out There tells us will make us happy. Yes, it seems that most people in the school car park listen to The World Out There and drive fancy expensive cars, and I choose to drive a tiny Honda Jazz. Do I fit in with the tribe? Absolutely not. But will that kill me? No. Does it threaten my basic needs? Nope. Yet my first feeling is one of shame, wanting to fight by justifying to the world why *I'm* right to not spend huge amounts of money on a car and then wheel-spin out of there, fleeing in shame.

From a brain science perspective, our upper, rational brain is only fully formed when we are twenty-five. This is the part of the brain that governs logic, thinks slowly and rationally, and is able to choose and moderate its response. It can override flight or fight, control our emotions, and keep things in perspective on a good day when it's energy-fuelled and we're fundamentally safe.

Until our brain is fully formed at age twenty-five, our primary source of behaviour control is the more primitive brain—the fight, flight, or freeze part, the safe-keeping part that uses and responds to fear and is so vulnerable to others who use fear to keep us within the tribe. It's why teenagers so desperately need to find a tribe and feel accepted somewhere and can fight an adult as if their lives were at stake. Because for them, they perceive that they are under threat.

Since so much of our identity is formed before we are twenty-five, our concept of who we believe we are is created before we actually have a fully-formed, upper rational brain to logically argue it out with that primitive brain of ours. We had no other choice but to accept as fact that child-like interpretation of the world—to believe what that nasty girl on the playground said about us or the words our tired parents or teachers yelled in a moment of weakness—because we couldn't talk sense to our broken heart.

Our Best Life Tree

To understand how your brain functions and impacts your Best Life, think of your Best Life as the biggest most beautiful tree in the middle of a gorgeous, lush garden.

The part you see above the surface is what everyone sees. The success, the fun, the work, the family, the outward health and wealth are all the leaves, flowers, and fruits of the tree.

They're supported by primary and secondary branches—your relationships; your spiritual, mental, and physical health; the hours you put into your work and managing your money; your learning and personal growth; giving back and engaging in a community.

In biology, this part of the tree above the tree trunk is called the crown—and in our Best Life, we wear a crown of the most beautiful jewels imaginable.

Best Life Tree

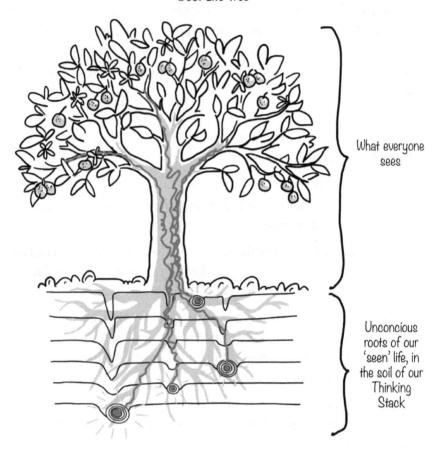

What everyone
sees

Unconcious
roots of our
'seen' life, in
the soil of our
Thinking
Stack

But the crown is only as healthy as the trunk that props it up and feeds and waters those leaves and flowers and fruit. The trunk is made up of the "Support Six," the essential components to support the beautiful tree of your Best Life. At the core is Thinking—affecting everything you do. Your Thinking is surrounded by Happiness, Health, Wealth, and Work. The outer layer, the bark of the tree, is Wisdom—our guide in this journey of life.

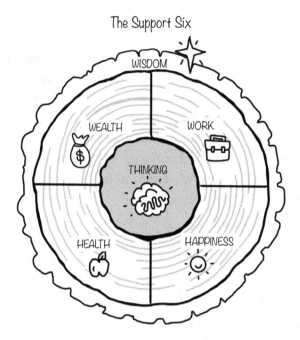

The Thinking core is the strength, the stability, and the food and water of your whole tree. Those thoughts go through from the roots in the soil to the fruit on the trees. Nothing exists without that central core. In the trunk, these thoughts are conscious—we know about them or at least can see their action through the rest of the tree above the ground.

But below the soil line is the subconscious—this huge matrix of deep roots that live below the surface of the ground and the soil. The only way you know it exists is through the fruit and leaves that show themselves above the surface in our behaviour and our conscious thoughts. When the garden of our lives looks beautiful and the crown has gorgeous leaves and flowers, we don't give a second thought to what's happening with the roots below. But every now and then, a branch of leaves dies or the fruit doesn't come that season, and we realize that things may not necessarily be as rosy as we thought they were. It may be time to go digging and examine the roots and the soil they live in. No conscious thought or action exists without deep roots in the Thinking Stack.

The soil the roots live in is the Thinking Stack. It's the part of the subconscious that just exists, made up of years and years of experiences, words, things we've seen. The roots are what link the subconscious soil to the crown of the tree at the top—the rising of subconscious thoughts into actions. The worms and weeds that poison our roots *love* the Deep Grooves of hurt, pain, and disappointment in our lives. If our soil is bad, the thoughts that initiate our actions are bad. And if our Thinking is bad, our trunk is weak. And if our trunk of Happiness, Health, Wealth, and Work is weak, the everyday fruits of our lives don't grow, and our tree becomes lonely, bare, desolate.

So it's crucial we understand our Thinking.

The Unwinnable Battle

In one of my podcast interviews with Dr. Abby Medcalf,[1] she mentioned that the conscious brain processes at fifty bits per second, but the subconscious brain processes at eleven million bits per second. When I heard this, it was as if the missing piece of the puzzle fell into place. There was no way I could ever simply will a behaviour change with my precious fifty bits of conscious logic if the full might of my eleven million bits of subconscious was going the opposite way. It would be like going solo into a battle with a stick against the full might of the world's best cavalry armed with the greatest weaponry ever conceived.

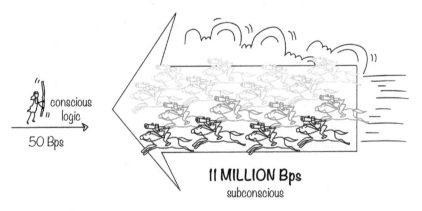

The Battle of the Consciousnesses

conscious logic

50 Bps

11 MILLION Bps
subconscious

It was then I knew I needed to find a way to locate and remove the weeds of faulty thinking in my subconscious, excavate below the surface, and remove their weedy roots. The problem was and still is, I'm not one for dwelling on the past. I'm terrible at touchy-feelies, and group care-and-share 'leadership' programs at work were my absolute worst. So I needed to develop a framework for myself that I could do in the safety of my introverted space at home without anyone else, the minute an issue arose.

Subconscious thinking is, by definition, below our conscious thinking, so the only way to change it is to start being mindful of our words and behaviours—the parts we see above the surface—and then look for deeper patterns. It's like stepping back and watching the movie of our life, where we look not only at what we do and say but as deeply at what we *don't* do or say, especially when we know we should have.

The Thinking Stack Framework gives us a tool to help us dig. Like the removal of any weeds, changing long-held thought patterns requires us to dig all the way to the bottom of the roots to ensure we examine and remove it all. You can't just try to deal with the leaves of the weed you see on the surface, because chopping it off will just result in it reappearing again and again in your life. Chopping at the leaves or weeds is just treating the symptom and not the cause.

The Reverse Thinking Stack

Essentially, we need to reverse engineer our Thinking Stack—starting from the top of the soil and moving downwards to the original groove, lump, or bump that caused our Thinking Stack to start developing weeds.

That's why I call it the "Reverse Thinking Stack."

What's causing us to feel like we do now?

1. Start with the **trigger**—that behaviour or thought that signals to us that it's not all hunky dory in the garden of life. For me, one signal is often the crushing, burning feeling in the middle of my chest of shame or some other sensation in my

body. When a thought or action is a trigger, it's almost always manifested physically in the fight, flight, or freeze response.

2. Then we need to head back into our earliest memory of a situation like that. What was the earliest **event** that we can remember that first happened that felt similar to the way we feel now? What happened and who was there?

What's going on below the surface?

3. We then look at the **assumptions** that we are making now. The story we're telling ourselves. Why did we assume potential harm or threat, or why were we drawn to potential opportunity? Why did we feel the need to protect or defend ourselves or want to run away and hide? Why did we dismiss that person, put them down, or feel the need to elevate ourselves? What made us link this event to the earliest event?

4. We then need to articulate the **feeling**. Brené Brown says our emotional literacy vocabulary is usually around 3–6 feelings, yet we have between 30–40 with 29 being core emotions.[2] Learn to discriminate between them, and be able to articulate your feelings more clearly. In particular, learn to focus on the difference between shame, guilt, humiliation, and embarrassment.

5. Close this section by articulating your overall response **instinct.** Do you want to fight? Or, using its twin, bitching to your friend—having the fight without the person there? Or are you just paralysed, freezing up and doing nothing? My most common reaction is the last one—flight. I love to dig my head in the sand and "run away," hoping the issue will resolve itself. My immediate response usually is to want to vent to John (fight), but as that settles, I move toward fleeing since I hate conflict, and hope it will go away.

Here's an example to help you see this process in action.

As I work toward my goal to teach one million women how to live their Best Lives and master their money, I feel that crushing sensation on my chest as I think about building a more public profile to spread the message. Why is my body signalling danger through shame?

Going through the Reverse Thinking Stack Framework with the acronym TEAFI (Trigger, Event, Assumption, Feeling, Instinct):

1. **Trigger** for thinking: I've become aware that I resist doing the weekly social media for my business, and when people refer to my posts, I want to run away and hide (flee). I get that crushing feeling on my chest.
2. **Earliest Event:** Being shouted at in public, ostracised, and publically suspended in pre-school for decorating my tribe.
3. **Assumption:** If I step in and "claim my space" of leadership in this online world, it's going to end up in pain, shame, and being banished. Don't do this and I am guaranteed to stay safe.
4. **Feeling:** The overwhelming feeling is one of shame.
5. **Instinct:** Flee. Run and hide. Step away from this car, it will explode.

Now I've done a lot of thinking on that one incident, which makes it easy to summarise so elegantly. You would need to be a true unicorn to come up with that in one go!

When I'm processing a situation that has, for example, made me extremely angry, I often have to go through the sequence a few times to get clarity on the differences between Good Reasons and Real Reasons, and dig further into the earliest events. Often, over time, I will see that my feelings and instinct change as I process the event and start to see beyond myself and towards the other person's feelings. But in the next chapters, I'll take you through how we dig to find the end point of that root.

THE Key You Need

But before we do, I need to give you *the* key to unlocking all of this.

It's a pen and paper.

I'm not joking.

Journaling is *the* key to understanding what's going on in your subconscious and why it's sabotaging you from making the changes you need to make to live your Best Life.

It's been proven to reduce stress, increase successful health outcomes when facing a scary hospital procedure, reduce consequent illness when used to write about traumatic or stressful events, and improve all round levels of happiness.[3] The best part about it is that psychologists have also proven that those who journal for fifteen minutes just three to five times in a four-month period can achieve these health and psychological benefits too.[4]

From James W. Pennebaker's seminal study on the field of Expressive Writing in 1986,[5] over 200 further studies that reference his work have confirmed not only the psychological but also the physical health benefits of journaling, including sleep, reduced blood pressure, and even a boost to the immune system observed by the body's physical lymphocyte or white blood cell response.

There are many reasons why it has such great benefits. Not only does it facilitate the opportunity for you to think through and reflect on your experiences, but it also uses many parts of your brain that just plain thinking doesn't. Writing is a left hemisphere task, which activates a different part of the brain than talking does and requires all those different muscles in your hand to translate thought into a character on the page. The sensation of the page under your hand, the visual cues of watching that page, and the work to access not only the memory of the event but also the analysis of the interpretation and assumptions means that you are far more engaged in the process.

But there's also a brain function called *encoding*. This is where our brain works out what we should discard and what we should remember. As we have our Ah-Ha moments, as we gain more clarity and rewrite the interpretations of an event, encoding helps us to start patching up that soil, getting rid of the weed's roots, and leaving it fertile for a beautiful plant of change to bloom.

The Active Learning Cycle

For me, there's another important reason why journaling my reflections is so important. In 1984, David Kolb published the Active or Experiential Learning Cycle,[6] which is how we as adults *should* learn in order to truly change our lives, work, or knowledge.

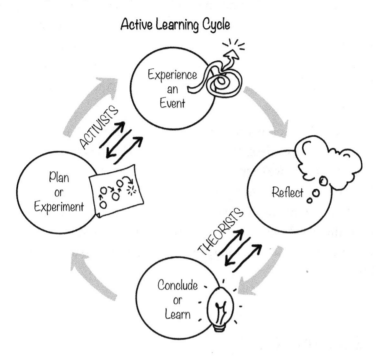

Active Learning Cycle

1. We have an experience.
2. After that, we should reflect on that experience, taking note of any inconsistencies between our experience and our understanding or assumptions.
3. We then decide how we should modify our understanding with the updated information and
4. Plan how to do things differently or even experiment with a new behaviour or thought process—like a new habit.

The challenge is most of us are not such wonderfully rounded, theoretically perfect learning creatures. We have a preferred style. Some are "Theorists"—people whose learning style preference is between reflecting and concluding, who tend to think and watch when they learn. On the other hand, I am an "Activist." I like to plan and do, spending my time experimenting and experiencing.

It's why I need to journal—I need to force my brain to reflect and then write down what I conclude my thinking should be so I learn from that behaviour (and not just have an Ah-Ha moment and head straight into planning my next move!). Because I'm a doer, I truly struggle to *just think*—be it in meditation, prayer, or problem solving. I find writing—my prayers, the answer to a question I'm struggling with, my business goals, or my gratitude "three things" (more on that later)—enables me to think them through, conclude and learn, and plan the next steps.

As I reflect on my own life and watch others' lives, there appears to be a Grand Canyon that exists between our goals, their execution, and the impact we're truly after. The intention to change—our behaviour, our thinking, our job, our health, our life—so often remains just that, an intention. If we want to make our intention a reality and have the effect we so deeply desire, then we need to use every tool we can to rewrite our interpretations and our assumptions that are holding us back.

JOURNALING

As we begin this journey, there's a workbook available that you can download at www.LisaLinfield.com/DeepGroovesDownload.

- Which part of the Kolb's Active Learning Cycle do you struggle most with?
- Take the most recent issue where you've experienced hurt, anger, shame, frustration or snapped at someone and regretted it later. Work through the steps of the Reverse Thinking Stack to get to the root of the issue.

3

The World Out There
Tells You Such Crap

I was a pretty ugly teenager. I was overweight and had some serious acne, and the benefits of makeup to hide the freckly face and provide that smooth, photoshopped magazine complexion were not available. I went to an all-girls boarding school, which I loved, but our interaction with the neighbouring boys' schools always required us to be in school uniform, free of makeup.

The excitement of the term were the socials held at the local boys' school. The challenge was that you had to be invited by a boy at that school to attend. This was fine when my brother was at one of the schools, but he was older than me, and he finished school two years before me. During my final two years, those invites from other boys never came. So I'd plaster a smile on my face, muster up all the fake excitement I could, and help my friends dress for their invite to the dance. I'd bravely wave them goodbye on the bus, wish them luck with the latest boy they wanted to hook up with, and then return to my dormitory bed, curl up in a ball, put a pillow over my head so no one would hear, and sob my eyes out.

The dating scene also had a domino effect of shifting alliances in friendships. You see, if you liked a guy whose sister was in your class, she suddenly became your new best friend. I had many of those, as my brother was just one of those delicious, charismatic humans who was both good-looking and in the cool group of guys. One minute you were ignored, and the next moment you were in the centre of the action. Similarly, your true friends would also disappear to spend time with others whose boyfriends or brothers were friends with their latest loves. And as the pretty girls always had the latest boyfriends . . . that was the way it rolled.

Pretty = boyfriend, friends, cool group

Ugly = lonely

As an adult, I giggle at how flaky the alliances were, how fluid the tribe dynamics flowed to ensure survival of the species. I see the hormones of teenagers dictating the flavour of the week. Yet as I look at that little girl curled up in a ball and sobbing on her boarding school bed, her rejection feels far more real to me than the adult logic I *know* to be the truth.

And I know, too, that that Deep Groove of thinking around the supremacy of being pretty is a belief I've adopted from The World Out There. It's formed such a deep hole in my soul that it has significantly impacted my self-confidence, my choice of environment, my feeling of belonging.

When I take the time to journal my thoughts, the beliefs I've formed from those early years are scary:

- You need to say the right thing and wear the right clothes in order to be cool and fit in.
- Sometimes you need to be mean to someone or talk behind their back in order to support the leader in her latest quest of putting someone down to make herself feel better. It's survival, and not doing so leads to you getting kicked out the tribe.
- Teachers are always right. People in authority are always right. Parents are always right. And therefore, you are wrong.
- Be a good girl so everyone is happy with you and life is easier.
- People who are clever and work hard will be top, the best.
- In order to make a living, you need to work seven days a week.
- You need to be skinny and look like Cindy Crawford with flawless skin, gorgeous hair, and Richard Gere next to you.

When I think back to the events that triggered these beliefs and the people who reinforced them, very few of them feel like "reliable sources."

The friends in primary school—where I learnt about trying to fit in, saying the right things, wearing the same clothes—may all be nice humans, but to be fair, it's thirty-five years later, and they shouldn't still be sitting in my head, telling me that I'm not cool enough or I need to say something to impress them.

The magazines of my days and the social media of today tell us what we should wear and how we should look, but the flawless skin they said we should have was all "air-brushed" in our day and photo-shopped or filtered now.

And as much as I truly believe teachers are saints, I also know how human they are, with their own insecurities and bad days. They're not always right, and like every one of us, there are days when they crave quiet because they have a headache. And if they tell you your latest idea is wrong, or shush you and tell you not to make suggestions or speak up, it's probably because a different approach is just too much effort for her after her own sleepless night.

These messages from our youth become the faulty landscape upon which our adult experiences grow. Being a good girl at school translates to being a good girl at work, and the praise you seek from that tired teacher becomes the praise you seek from your tired boss.

The Faulty Landscape of Gender

Your worldview and social context are crucial lenses of step two in the Reverse Thinking Stack, interpretation of the event. We absorb all these inputs from The World Out There, magnified by the time in history, our economic background, our homes and families.

Like most of us, I grew up at a time when The World Out There taught me that men were better than women. That was the social context of the '70s, '80s, and '90s. Despite my mum working my whole life and running a very successful business, she still conformed to the norm that she would then have dinner on the table by the time my dad came home.

I grew up with the stories of amazing women in my family, because I come from an impressive lineage of matriarchal achievers. Unfortunately for them, their husbands died early in their lives, leaving them with young children and the need to step up and provide for them. These circumstances forced them to defy the social stereotyping of their day that women were seen and not heard. They slayed social norms, took on governments, ran businesses. They were land barons, mayors, fishing-rod business owners, honorary-doctorate holders, and founding members of the Suffragette movement in the UK and the Black Sash in South Africa—all fighting for the rights of women.

Yet I also grew up with the views of The World Out There seeping into my soul and impacting my interpretation and assumptions of every event:

- Men become CEOs; women are secretaries.
- Women are emotional, weak, and erratic.
- Men become successful at work; women stay at home and raise the children. Those who don't are not good mothers.
- Men make the money; women spend it.
- Girls look after and care for everyone.
- Ladies need to be petite and pretty to find a good husband who will care for them.
- Women are not equal. If you want to be, you must fight for your space.
- Logic is king. Men are logical. Men are king. Women are emotional. Men win.

When I asked my community about what The World Out There tells them about men and women, not much seems to have changed, despite all the work we've done as a society.

- Andrew's response made me giggle: *Yoh! That's a big question! Men and women are completely equal, but men do the heavy lifting! So do we naturally look to women for mental and moral support? I think so.*

- Lachelle, a talented finance director with children who are now just out of university, told me this: *The workplace still does not understand or cater for the demands of motherhood and a career.*
- The financial inequality and access to opportunity still raises its ugly head in Michelle's comment: *Woman are paid less than men for the same job and there are very few women in decision-making positions in the IT industry.*
- And these worldviews are not just things of the past or the present—my twelve-year-old responded to the question saying: *A woman needs to work twice as hard to get half as far.*

My own experience in the corporate world mirrored the prejudices of The World Out There. I was most often the only woman in a team of men and had a double prejudice in my twenties and thirties of being the youngest in senior leadership by several years. When I was twenty-five in the UK in the early 2000s, I sat on the executive team of a six-million-pound business. Every month we would take two days out and go to a hotel to have a strategy day. It amazed me how often people in the hotel would assume I was the secretary and ask me what time we wanted lunch. Those comments, whilst odd, didn't really impact me as I was far more insecure about my age than my gender.

Rewriting the Gender Stereotype

I look back and realise how exceptionally lucky I was that my husband John and I essentially earned the same amount until I gave up corporate to start my own business. It gave us a container to explore these long-held stereotypes of The World Out There so ingrained in the fibre of both our bodies.

Both of us had grown up with mums at home. When we had no kids and were earning nicely, the stereotypical roles weren't an issue. We'd share the cooking or get heat-up meals from the supermarket.

However, when I was on maternity leave and working only half-day, most of the home and baby chores fell on me. It was logical, but it also surprised me how quickly we reverted to what we had seen. When I went back to full-day working, things remained that way, and for a few weeks I felt my resentment grow beneath the surface. We were both working full days, both earning the same, both having equal responsibility, yet I was shouldering the burden of all the home and children chores. On our first date night after my return to working full day, I raised the topic, but there seemed no obvious, easy way to divide the chores.

Our next date night, I went with a proposal. I hate shopping and cooking. John hates admin and the way it forces him to think about calling the plumber or the gate man when he is at work and wants to focus 100 percent on work. Now whilst admin is in no way my gift either, I can at least do it. So we agreed that in our house, John would shop on the weekend and cook when our home helper didn't. That was his responsibility. And I would take care of the admin around the girls' schedules, the home maintenance, our investments, and life in general. It's not a fifty-fifty division of every single task, but it's a fair division and works for us.

Hopefully, our rewriting of the gender stereotype—not only in word but in action—will counter the historic perspective for our three girls. How else does it change if we don't show the boys and girls we care for a different way?

Examining the Guilt

Working full day also meant that John and I had to share the girls' activities at school. I couldn't make it to all their functions due to work commitments, so right from the beginning he also had to carve time out, cancel meetings, and make sure he showed up. I struggled to adjust to this, as I suffered mummy's guilt about not being able to attend everything—as my mum and all the mums when I grew up had done.

I never knew I held that belief deeply until the first ballet show I was unable to attend. Before then, it was easy to *say* that mums and dads should share the load—never once thinking that I myself would struggle with the guilt of that concept.

Years of journaling and consciously practicing Kolbe's Active Learning Cycle have forced me to reflect on the guilt of not being able to attend every event and of sharing the load with John. I realized I needed to come to a different conclusion and practice better behaviour. And after eight years of this work, I now deeply believe with all my soul that it *is* better for children to have both their parents step in—together and by themselves—to show up for them, make the dinner, shop, and catch the balls of life in a partnership. And I love that I can live that example for my girls . . . when I stop to reflect. In the moment, it mostly feels like I'm dropping balls left, right, and centre!

The Wisdom of Age

I have always loved the wisdom of age, and I consider myself extremely privileged to have spent three years living with my gran when I was at university. Not only did I get to know her deeply as a human (not just a gran), but I also got to learn so much from her reflections on current affairs and my own challenges of growing up. Once, we were watching the news together on the TV when she spoke a comment so profound, it's never left me.

"Darling," she said, "we did well to fight for the equal rights of women, to teach them that they can do anything a man can do if they choose. But where we fell short is that we forgot to teach the men about how to respond to a world where women are equal to men."

The insight in that statement is profound, coming from a woman who was a founding member of the Black Sash and fought so hard for minority's rights and in particular, their right to vote.

To truly change the world requires *both* parties to deeply engage in shifting the story The World Out There tells us *and* match their behaviour to support that. It requires role models on both sides showing the generations to come what it means to step into the new way of being. Yes, it does start by changing the way we think—but what we often miss is that it's through our *actions* that the next generation will understand our change in thinking. To truly change The World Out There's thinking, we have to completely remodel our interpretations and assumptions and the deep frameworks of our thinking through reflection. I'm so grateful to John for living this example to our daughters every day.

Changing the world and changing ourselves to live our own Best Life requires new definitions of right and wrong, strong and weak, brave and cowardly, and what gives us true happiness and security. To change our behaviour, we need to dig below the Good Reasons, easy assumptions, and habitual behaviour and do the work to find the *Real Reasons*. If not, we will continue to seek short-term hits of worldly happiness in an attempt to fill the hole in our soul.

JOURNALING

When it comes to each of the following, what did The World Out There tell you? Write your deepest instinctual response, not the 'good answers.' Some thinking prompts:

- The role of a man and a woman
- The work men and women do
- Physical looks
- Money
- Caring for others
- Work
- "Good" work and "bad" work
- "Good" girls/boys and "bad" girls/boys

4

Short-Term Hits of Happiness

I've always said that I will judge a smoker unable to give up smoking when I have successfully given up sugar. Chocolate and ice cream are my most delicious vices and can end any good intention I may have of a healthy week. Heaven is going to have tubs of Triple Caramel Ice Cream stashed *everywhere*—slightly melty and gooey.

My biggest trigger for eating sugar is tiredness. When I'm tired, I just want that hit of sugar for its short-term spike of energy and happiness. As a result, afternoons and evenings—or any day following too little sleep—are my worst times for giving into sugar.

When I think of Triple Caramel Ice Cream, I totally understand addictive behaviour. If it's in the fridge, I can be innocently watching TV, and it starts to call me seductively from the freezer—"Lisaaah. Liiiiiissssaaaaaahhhhhhhhhh"—until it's drilling a hole in my head. And then, like one of those cartoon characters, I start to get up from the sofa in a trance and walk toward the freezer, despite my angel-voice saying, "Do *not* do it."

"Do not walk there."

"Do not open the fridge door."

"OK, whatever you do, do not take out the ice-cream box."

"OK, whatever you do, limit it to one scoop."

"OK, I give up."

And before you know it, that bowl has been demolished—despite knowing with every fibre of my body that sugar and me just truly don't go well together. I know tomorrow I will feel low in energy and like an elephant's sitting on my sinuses. And I also know that the guilt of giving in will cause me to be beat myself up, non-stop for at least a day. But in that moment, that release of the happy hormone, dopamine, and the spike of energy feels *so* worth it.

The shadow side of "short-term hits of happiness" is that we use them to numb ourselves. When my world is higgledy-piggledy and I can't even tell you why, I can switch on that TV and stay watching *long* after my body has told me to go to bed. And like the ice-cream battle in my brain, my "Still Small Voice" says, "Come now, friend, you're shattered—let's go to bed," at the exact same time my hands load the next episode in the series.

The Hit of Praise and Giving

Short-term hits of happiness don't only take the form of the usual suspects—drugs, alcohol, cigarettes, sex, sugar, and food.

Another more subtle short-term hit of happiness for me is being the overachieving, good little girl, the perfect people-pleaser. It feels good when someone praises your work, tells you what a good girl you are. One modern equivalent is social media likes or, for me, podcast downloads.

Praise gives you that exact same wonderful dopamine release as sugar, the happy hormone we all crave. And over time, that praise re-enforces the message that The World Out There tells us—be liked, be good, and receive praise, because that's what will make you happy.

Another one I see a lot is giving. I know, it sounds weird to put that in the short-term hits of happiness category. But for all of us, giving gives us the "feel good" factor. Giving, especially in women, releases oxytocin—another happy hormone. Again, this re-enforces The World Out There's mantra that it is "better to give than receive."

But for those that use giving to fill the hole in the soul, they find themselves giving everything—themselves, their money, their time, or their body—for that short-term hit of happiness. The happiness that comes from seeing the smile on the face of the receiver is the best hit of giving. But in its shadow grows a resentment that it feels like no one ever reciprocates, that the scales aren't balanced, that they're being taken advantage of.

It's not limited to giving in a charitable or social context. You see it at work, especially in the "giving or helping" service professions. As much as it feels good in the moment to give your products or services away for a cheap rate or for free in the name of helping others, over time it ends up in resentment—resentment that you don't have enough money to send your kids to a good school, that you're working overtime, or that people and clients don't value the work you do and take advantage of you.

Sometimes that resentment comes from the deep belief of sacrificial giving. Other times it's not as clear as that. It's why just looking at the superficial Good Reasons for going after short-term hits of happiness will never help you solve or address the Real Reasons.

The Real Problem behind Short-Term Hits

All the short-term hits of happiness are perfect in small, balanced amounts—*balance* being the operative word. The shadow side of any form of happiness is when we become dependent on it as a replacement for deep, genuine joy. No matter how much we throw short-term hits of happiness at the deep-genuine-joy hole in our souls, it will never be able to fill it. Ask an addict if they have a genuine, deep sense of joy, and, like the people-pleaser, they will tell you that in the moment it feels good, but despite how hard they try, that good feeling is never long term and is not deeply fulfilling joy.

All hits of happiness make us feel, for that short time, like our problems disappear, our heart is happy, we're slaying the dragons, and conquering the world. In that moment, we feel in control, like we are the ones choosing on the playground. *We* have done something that results in this happiness. That happiness feels especially fulfilling when our world often feels completely out of *control*. With that little hit, for one brief moment we put our stake firmly in the ground and stop the world from whizzing around us. That sense of control, of energy, of happiness, and of acceptance is what makes those short-term hits of happiness so addictive. It's almost the physical YAY! after the emotional beating up we've given ourselves for our latest mess-up. As we do it again and again, it starts to make an easy groove of false happiness we seek more often, deepening the groove and making it even harder to get out of it.

What's so destructive is that over time, short-term hits of happiness destroy our belief in ourselves—that we can resist it—which deepens the hole in our soul. That high we get from all hits of happiness starts to dwindle. Its ability to release that same level of happy hormones gets smaller and smaller. That once craved-for car becomes the default option as we seek the next bigger and brighter one. The praise from your boss becomes normal and you seek it from their boss now. The feeling from one drink only starts to kick in after four.

This type of happiness comes from something outside of us, an *external source*. And its aftereffects just worsen the hole in our soul. We beat ourselves up for doing something our angel-voice knew we shouldn't do in the first place, and the Cruella de Vil–voice in our heads berates us over the monthly repayments (with interest), the scale in the bathroom and additional fatigue, the hangover from drink or the withdrawal from drugs, the pile of work that never got done because we were watching TV.

Cruella keeps me small, ashamed, and fearful. She finds any opportunity to point out where I've gone wrong and what a bitch I am, and how far short I am from The World Out There's picture of happiness. Short-term hits of happiness are her absolute feeding ground.

Short-Term Hits of Happiness

T.W.O.T

So you work hard and do well

But over time

You work harder to achieve more...

Success = Happiness

Which makes you happy, so T.W.O.T must be right

The hole in your soul widens as the rush becomes the new normal

Over time: Leads to unhappiness

Finding happiness inside yourself is hard, messy, and takes a lot of work and time to separate out the Good Reasons and Real Reasons we reach for the quick fix.

The Reason We Undercharge for Our Work

When I first started my financial planning business, I decided I would charge R10–R15,000 (the buying power equivalent of $1–1,500) for my financial plans, depending on the complexity. For the first twenty months of my business, I mostly gave them away for free. The good reason I told myself was that I was just starting out, I needed to build experience, this was my "school fees." But over time it got to a stage where I knew that whilst that may be a good reason, it was not in fact the real reason. And I would soon be both broke and even more resentful if I didn't start charging a fair price for my work.

I did some deep soul searching around this topic, and, as usually happens when we open ourselves up to find answers, God sends them in many forms. One was an article by Scott Mautz, who said that we lower how much we're worth in order to chase the approval of others. If they say yes, we feel elated for that brief moment because they "approved"—we get the short-term hit of happiness. But inside it niggles at us because we're disappointed that we didn't have the guts to ask for what we're worth. We know the trade of our service for their money wasn't fair.

What makes it worse is when they say no at the discounted rate. We are crushed because we believe they're telling us that not only are we not worth what they should be paying, we're not even worth the discounted rate.

As I thought deeply about this, I realized that in my case this was the Real Reason. I have a huge fear of failure and rejection, of not being chosen on the playground. In addition, I'm unable to ask for what I'm worth because I so want to win the approval of other people—the short-term hit of happiness of them saying yes.

When they said no, I felt they were personally rejecting me as a human being, that they didn't like me or think that I was worth that amount of money. I concluded that I was definitely not good enough and I had failed. They didn't choose me for their team.

Planning a New Way Forward

So how do we find out what the Real Reasons are that we're seeking short-term hits of happiness?

Take out your pen and your journal, and go through the steps of the Reverse Thinking Stack. Remember the acronym T-E-A-F-I: Trigger, Event, Assumption, Feeling, Instinct. When we start to look at behaviour we want to change, we then add two extra layers to the Reverse Thinking Stack: Wisdom and Action.

Wisdom: We all draw on wisdom from somewhere—it could be books, mentors, parental teaching. For me, my wisdom comes from my faith. If I'm truly to think and therefore behave in a completely aligned manner, I need to continuously draw my faith into my action. But for every one of us—we need to tap into that Still Small Voice of Wisdom that is our good angel, our better version of ourselves. I've had times when my entire Thinking Stack, including Action, is filled with anger at a person or situation. But the simple act of writing down what Wisdom says about this situation connects me to the better side of my humanity and plants the seed in amongst the anger of a different path. I also write here what my gut is telling me, to try and get more in tune with it (more on this later).

Action: What is the action you will take? Planning the new way of being is crucial to changing our habits, doing things differently. And then, making sure you do it! One of the keys here is to start planning from when you are triggered. For example: The next time someone says . . . I will then . . .

So let me take you through the Reverse Thinking Stack I used for my example:

What caused me to feel like I did?

1. The **Trigger** for thinking was finding myself offering my service for free or discounting it—not charging what I'm worth for my service. This always made me feel uncomfortable, and if they said no to the discounted rate, the crushing elephant sat on my chest.

2. The **Event** way back when came from those many times at junior school when I wasn't chosen on the playground, and in high school when no boys asked me out.

What's going on below the surface?

3. The **Assumption** was that if someone says no, they were rejecting me as a human being, and *I* wasn't good enough for them to pay. The story I told myself was that nobody liked me and that I was unlovable, because I wasn't chosen.

4. The **Feelings** were deep rejection, sadness, loneliness, isolation, unworthiness and shame.

5. My **Instinct** was to hide, to flee the circumstances. More often than not, I'd concede and give it for free just to hear them say yes—so desperate was I to get rid of those feelings and replace it with a short-term hit of happiness.

How can I do things differently?

6. **Wisdom** says in Isaiah 41:9: "I took you from the ends of the earth, from its farthest corners I called you . . . *I have chosen you and have not rejected you.*" And, "See, I have engraved you on the palms of my hands." Not only am I loved by the Creator, He chose me. Does it really matter who else in The World Out There chooses me if God has already? My gut (and research) also tells me that my price is fair and my product is excellent—no matter what the voice in my head says.

7. **Action**—learn to live with the silence, the pause that comes after saying my fee. It's uncomfortable, but don't immediately discount it. You've done your homework, Lisa, your rate is at the low end of the market, and your work is good. And if they

say "No," it's NOT an indication of you as a person, or even your service (they haven't tried it!), it's no to the product, not no to Lisa the human.

I'm learning now that that short-term hit of happiness for people saying yes to my service at a reduced rate is in fact destroying my sense of self-worth in the long term. Exactly the same as an eating or drinking binge does.

I'm learning to live with the awkwardness of voicing my rate and living with the silence as they accept or decline it—and learning to fix the smile on my face in the pause!

I'm practicing separating Lisa the product from Lisa the human and learning to move on if they do say "no"—reminding myself that there are many reasons people say "no" that may have nothing to do with Lisa the human or my lovability.

Although so many of us were brought up on the old adage "it is better to give than receive," it's a concept I think we all need to get rid of. I'm all about the *AND*. We need to learn *both* to give *and* to receive— to allow others to give to us and just say "Thank you" in response. Receiving love in its many forms allows the balance of exchange to flow between two humans, and when that happens, true love can be present. Short-term hits of happiness are never true love, nor are they a fair trade of work or effort.

When We Screw Up

I was lucky enough to work for the most amazing boss during the latter portion of my career. We just clicked. Our values and our work ethic aligned, and we would laugh so much as he called me out on my crap.

One day I messed up something at work, so I went into his office, told him about it, and let him know what I was going to do to fix it. He just sat and listened. After a while, I asked him, "Saks, why aren't you shitting on me?"

His answer was so enlightening.

"Because I know that no one can beat you up more than you can beat yourself up."

And he was right. Before, during, and after that conversation I took that whip and beat myself up. I live every single day with my worst critic, telling myself the worst stories about who I am and my self-worth.

I remember once being asked, "Would you let *anyone* speak to your daughters the way you speak to yourself?" The more mindful I am, listening to what I say—especially when I mess up or give in to numbing myself with TV or that entire box of ice cream, the more I know that if anyone spoke to my girls like that, I'd hunt them down and throttle them!

The good little overachieving girl *hates* to mess up, hates to see the disappointment in the eyes of person affected by my mess up. That shame-elephant comes and sits on my chest and engulfs me. And my self-talk spirals into some of the meanest and nastiest words I can come up with.

You're useless.

You screwed up—again.

You're such an idiot.

Yet if one of my little girls messed up and told me they were thinking like that, I'd pull them close, give them a huge hug, tell them how proud I was that they gave it a try, and once they'd calmed down, I'd work with them to find out how they could do it differently next time.

Wanting to fit into The World Out There's definition of happiness, of right and wrong, of good and bad is natural. It's the tribal instinct in every one of us. But for the most part, it is unattainable, which leads us to feel that gap in our souls. And the gap leads us to seek short-term hits of happiness.

They will *never* fill the hole in our soul.

We trade that short-term hit of happiness for deep peace in our soul—an expensive price to pay for a moment of happiness or numbing. Yet because solving the root cause is so hard, and the hits so easy to find, we just keep ourselves "in control," "energy stacked," and "happy." Way, way easier.

Yet we are neither in control, nor enjoying lasting energy, nor experiencing deep joy.

So the question we need to ask ourselves is whether The World Out There's definition of happiness is truly something we should take as the standard? Should all those well-meaning teachers and adults and not so well-meaning little people at school, marketing companies, and insecure humans on Twitter truly be the basis of our thinking, our actions, and our lives?

JOURNALING

- What do you use as your short-term hits of happiness?
- Think about the last time you used your short-term hit of happiness. Go through your Reverse Thinking Stack Framework, and work out what triggers are at play and what assumptions you're telling yourself. Remember to tap into your source of Wisdom and what your gut says, and plan what Action you should take when you are next triggered.
- If you go to www.LisaLinfield.com/DeepGroovesDownload, you can download the Reverse Thinking Stack Framework (TEAFIWA) to keep with you as you journal.

5

Assumptions Become
Our Identity

From our earliest childhood years, our identity is shaped by all these faulty standards The World Out There sets us and our evaluation of how we stack up against them. If we can perform better than the standard, that becomes a positive part of our identity, and if we judge ourselves worse than what the teacher, parent, bully, or photoshopped social media says—well then that becomes a negative part of our identity. But the shadow side is that it also becomes an expectation we place on ourselves; if we fall short of it, it becomes a rod we use to beat ourselves.

These beliefs are ingrained deep in our subconscious and are expressed through our thinking and behaviour via two 2-word statements, "I am" and "I can." Or their opposites, "I'm not" or "I can't."

As I watch my daughter Jess navigate life, I'm one step removed but deeply invested, and I reflect on my own childhood. I wonder how much of my subconscious operating system is so deeply flawed because it's based on the interpretations of a young, hurt human living in the brutal world of children and teenagers.

I know there's a school of thought that believes our sense of self comes mainly from our First Loves—our parents and siblings. I agree that our family is our first tribe and foundational in our sense of self. But as children become independent and try to find their place in their own tribe at school, the influence of that tribe impacts their developing identity more and more. The relative influence of their first family tribe reduces as they seek the approval and position in their new tribal hierarchy of school friends.

The new circumstances give our Thinking Stacks more events to layer which our parents don't participate in, more opportunities to incorrectly interpret assumptions, and a variety of different worldviews from other families that all impose new assumptions on us.

Whilst I believe my daughter has a great sense of humour, her current identity statement is *I am **not** funny*. Why? Although she feels safe in her tribe at home, the tribe she wants to fit in most with is the school tribe. Some events there have led her to interpret that her joke or response wasn't funny, and she's incorporating that into her identity. When I tell her she *is* funny, she sometimes even assumes I am lying—because what I say contradicts this new primary tribe of hers. Mum is just the safe, default option. So her Thinking Stack that led her to initially think I *am* funny gets overwritten by a new subconscious Thinking Stack of I *am not* funny, and an assumption that it's safer not to crack a joke because she won't suffer the hurtful looks of others, won't feel rejected from the tribe. At best, she still holds on to the fact that to her mum, she's still hysterically funny.

It doesn't matter how much we want to logically will a behaviour change; it never will win unless we fundamentally change our life-long "I am" and "I'm not" and "I can" and "I can't" beliefs.

I had an epiphany about this in my own life regarding my personal exercise routine.

I had been exercising twice a week for seven years after I started paying for a personal trainer to hold me accountable. I always say that if you want to change something or get something done, you need to ensure that you do two things: get an accountability partner, and invest enough money either in learning or in that accountability partner that it hurts your pocket when you don't meet your commitments. It shifted the conversation in my head from "Do I feel like training?" (the answer to that is *never* yes) to "Do I feel like wasting the money I paid my trainer?" (and the answer is almost always, *no!*).

If you met a person who exercised twice every single week for seven years, would you say that they are a consistent and regular exerciser?

Most people would answer, "Yes."

Even though I was consistently exercising, the challenge was I would never in a million years say that I'm a consistent, regular exerciser.

You see, for most of my formative life, I could never stick consistently to exercising. I'd start for three or four weeks and give it up. Even though I played on sports teams my whole school and university life, that was more about fitting in and belonging to the team then it was about the enjoyment of the sport itself. It didn't translate well to the individual exercising for health we do as adults.

I also would never say that I exercised regularly because somewhere at medical school a regular exerciser was "a person who did more than four sessions of exercise per week." And back then, I believed that that was what you needed to do in order to be healthy—an all or nothing approach. So my subconscious identity, when it came to exercise, was I *am* a loser. I can't get myself to exercise consistently. I *am not* a regular exerciser, and I'm definitely not self-motivated.

Another story I had absorbed from The World Out There was that the only reason you would possibly exercise outside of a team sport was to lose weight while you dieted. I have always struggled with my weight, and in my twenties I gave up dieting. I subscribe to healthy eating and living a healthy life, just not to dieting. But because I wasn't dieting, exercise seemed pointless because that story was deeply embedded in my subconscious.

And then came my enlightening Ah-Ha moment.

For the last seven years, I had fought with myself before every single gym session. "Should I? Shouldn't I? Do I think I can miss? No. Yes. No." My eleven million bits of subconscious deeply believed that I *was not* a regular, consistent, self-motivated exerciser and so stubbornly refused to embrace the practice. In addition, my subconscious held onto the belief that if I *was not* on diet, and I *was not* interested in losing weight, I *should not* be doing this exercise thing. Plus, for years I told myself I *was not* an early riser because, like all teenagers,

I struggled to get up early. So waking up early was never going to be all right.

Needless to say, the fifty bits of logic that were telling me that I should exercise because I'm committed to my long-term health were little sticks of hope fighting a losing battle against the most powerful army of eleven million bits of subconscious identity statements that told me I shouldn't.

Fortunately for me, my money-brain overrode all this chaos. I was not going to waste the money I paid every single month for my trainer. So I told those eleven million bits of subconscious, "Full stop, be quiet. Every single thought of you out there, get back in your box. It's paid for, we're doing it."

And that's when it struck me: the key to changing your behaviour lies in the power of changing your subconscious identity. It's why it doesn't matter how much logic and good intentions we may have; we cannot will ourselves to change. Our New Year's resolutions will remain just that—intentions.

For the first time, I understood how I saw myself and how the statements I believed so deeply needed to change in order to successfully install the new habits that I wanted for my better life.

The next morning, I began to implement some short, quick affirmations (more on that later) that were backed up by the facts I knew to be true.

- I am a consistent, regular exerciser.
- I love how strong I feel after seven years of regular exercise.
- I am an early riser.

Over the next few weeks, I worked harder in my training sessions because for the first time, my subconscious wasn't fighting my being there with all its eleven million bits of power. I was aligned in subconscious, conscious, and action. My tree stood strong and congruent.

Since then, I have become so much more aware of when I want to change a behaviour and am struggling to do it. I use my Reverse

Thinking Stack exercises to work out what my I *am* and I *can* statements must be that are causing me not to make this change.

When Your Behaviour Is Incongruent with Your Goals

For two years I've known that there are four major ways that I can achieve my goal of teaching one million women about money. These would enable me to earn some income to pay for the costs of running the free side of the business that achieves those goal—the blogs, podcasts, videos.

1. I need to build and sell courses.
2. I need to write this book to get my message out.
3. I need to do more speaking.
4. I need to build partnerships with people who can help recommend my work. In order to do that, I need to get myself "out there"—raise my profile, get on radio and TV, focus on building a sales pipeline, approach companies and speaking agents for speaking opportunities.

But, I find myself struggling to do these things I know I need to. When my behaviour is incongruent with my goals over a prolonged period of time, I know I need to look at my thinking, because it's clear that some huge army is fighting my good intentions and logical strategy. I know I need to acknowledge that the thoughts I'm aware of are just the tip of the tree, that the lack of flowers, the empty branches, and the weeds in my garden point to the presence of the deep root system below that's not aligned with my intentions. That's when I find the Real Reasons my intention is not becoming my reality:

- What if I put myself out there through marketing or an agent and no one buys my course, buys my book, or wants me to speak?

- What if I speak on live TV or Radio and mess it up completely?
- What if they do buy but don't like what I do?
- What if they say no if I approach them directly?
- I *am* a useless salesperson. I *can't* sell.
- I *am* never chosen. Therefore no one will choose me as a speaker or choose my courses.
- I *am* an imposter—not as good as all those others out doing it already. I don't belong amongst them—they are all so talented.
- I *am* useless. I shouldn't even try . . .
- So if I don't try . . . then they won't say no . . . then I won't get rejected.

All these thoughts led to my decision to significantly discount my speaking and courses or offer them for free—all to minimise the risk of people saying no . . . *again*! I should have learnt this lesson after doing the same thing in my wealth management business.

Yet I know my courses are very good and over deliver the value in relation to the cost, and I've been speaking to large audiences since I was in Toastmasters at school. My most recent speech had such an impact on the audience, people were crying during the speech, and for an hour and a half after, people queued to speak with me.

No matter how much my logic tells me that my product is good enough, that people have their own reasons for not buying that may have *nothing* to do with me, my subconscious tells me the opposite. My screwed-up identity statements take any "no" as confirmation of their accuracy of my own worthlessness. "See, I told you so."

When I was early in the process of selling my course "Business School for Startups—The 16 Week Side Hustle," I sold only three—against a target of ten. I wanted to physically crawl under my desk, grip my knees close to my body, and hide after that final webinar. The vulnerability of being out there, of spending an hour "selling" when in fact I was teaching for free, of waging war with my baby fifty bits of logic against the full might of every one of those eleven million bits of subconscious—and then of receiving an answer that reinforced those negative assumptions just felt completely overwhelming. There is nothing more I wanted to do except hide—from exhaustion, disappointment, and a feeling of utter failure.

Logic Can Never Beat Identity

I see it all the time in my wealth management business. People tell themselves, "I'm useless at maths, so I'm useless at money. I can't do money. I'm too dumb to understand money. Women don't do money, I am a woman, therefore I can't do money." And what happens? Your subconscious makes sure you don't do money, struggling each day just to make ends meet or earning a lot, but never managing it in a way that enables you to be financially free.

When you tell yourself that "rich people become rich by being mean and selfish," you will never accumulate wealth, as your subconscious won't let you become one of those mean and selfish people. When people tell themselves that "all nice people help others," they end up unable to afford their own retirement because they've spent a lifetime giving all their money away to charities, their children, their friends. They end up needing to be supported in their old age by different charities, their children, and their friends who did manage to save—making them a taker and not a giver which becomes soul-destroying for them.

The stories you tell yourself become your deeply held identity. And if over a long period of time you're unable to make money, unable to hold onto it or unable to invest it—it's because there's something you're believing that's causing that. The tree of your life cannot have the roots and trunk of an apple tree, yet produce the fruits of an orange. It just doesn't work that way.

The problem is, when we discover these assumptions, excavate them, and dust them off, when we challenge ourselves to find out where they come from, who told us that, how we came to believe it so deeply, we find the source almost always is a flawed, hurt human, reinforced by the brain's prehistoric design to keep us safe from hurt and pain. Until we change them, we are never able to live our Best Life.

But nothing in life is fixed and permanent. We are not the same human today as we were thirty years ago, not the same as we were last year or even yesterday. Our experiences shape and mould us; each day we grow and change. Only once we know our assumptions and the identity statements we truly hold—and see them for what they are— then we'll be able to change them.

Did it hurt when so few people bought my course? Yes. Did I want to shelve the course and never think about it again? Absolutely. Every cell in my body wanted to flee to the safety of not selling my course, so no one could say no. But will I keep doing it? Absolutely. I believe it has the power to change people's lives by teaching them in a simple, easy-to-understand way how to start a business they can grow over time that will give them the financial and personal freedom their soul so desperately seeks.

The Back-to-Back Thinking Stack

So I have the choice of interpretation and assumption. I call this a Back-to-Back Thinking Stack process. Thinking Stack One is the set of interpretations that are "instinctive," that my bruised ego and broken soul want to indulge in, that Cruella wants to use to beat me up. But I force myself to do Thinking Stack Two: to move myself from the primitive brain's fight, flight, or freeze response to leveraging the power of my human brain, my fully-formed, reasonable, logical brain so that I don't lay down another stack on the Deep Groove of shame in my brain. An extra "I" is now added to our Reverse Thinking Stack—the I of the Identity Statements I'm believing.

Thinking Stack One:

What causes me to feel like I do now?

1. **Trigger:** Sales were disappointing, lower than what I expected them to be. In fact, they were hideously low.
2. **Earliest Event:** It is exactly like being 16 again and not getting invited to the dance.

What's going on below the surface?

3. **Assumption** (the story I'm telling myself): This will never work. No one likes me. No one chooses to do my course. My course is useless. I'm useless. You see, my brain is right, this was a stupid idea. Who am I to think I could enter this space of online courses?
4. **Feeling:** Rejection, shame, unworthiness, imposter syndrome.
5. **Instinct:** Give up. Run away. Hide.
6. **Identity Statement:** I *am* a useless sales person. I *am* never chosen. I *can't* ever be successful in this teaching space.

How can I move forward in a different way?

7. **Wisdom:** I'm sure there is some, but right now, I can't even think, I feel so much shame.
8. **Action:** I'm just going to shelve this course, and I'll write another one. Move along to the next shiny thing that I'm sure will work.

If I am to be real with myself, I need to be real in my Reverse Thinking Stack. It is crucial for me to be honest. You cannot change a thing if it's based on the way we think we should be, the Good Reasons, a fake mask.

Sometimes it will take me days before I even open my journal and get to Thinking Stack Two if I'm really hurt, angry, or feeling deep shame. Other times, I will do it immediately afterward because I know I'm just lashing out.

Thinking Stack Two:

You will notice that the event and trigger are the same—they always will be. But what changes is the assumptions we're making and our interpretation of the event.

What causes me to feel like I do now?

1. **Trigger:** Sales were disappointing, lower than what I expected them to be. In fact, they were hideously low.
2. Earliest **Event:** I acknowledge my heart is feeling the same type of rejection I did when I was sixteen and wasn't invited to the dance.

What's going on below the surface?

3. **Assumption** (the story I *need to be* telling myself): This is not even in the same universe as not getting invited to the dance, let alone time zone. This is just going to need a lot more work than I thought, and I'm lucky to have this learning, this data, that shows me where I need to improve. You're just starting out. It takes a lot of time to build trust with people so that they will buy. In fact, science shows that most people need to experience the offer more than seven times in order to buy. This is the first. Nothing great was ever an instant success. It's not you personally; it just takes time, learning, persistence.
4. **Feeling:** Bruised, but not beaten. Knocked down, but not out the ring.
5. **Instinct:** Weary, but resisting the desire to flee. Pick yourself up and plan the next launch.
6. **Identity:** I *am* just starting out. I *can* do this.

How can I move forward in a different way?

7. **Wisdom:** "I can do all this through him who gives me strength" (Philippians 5:13). I know I feel I don't have the strength to pick myself up and head back into the arena for another round of selling this course . . . but somehow God will give me the strength. "Have I not commanded you? Be

strong and courageous, do not be discouraged, for the Lord your God will be with you wherever you go" (Joshua 1:9). I deeply believe that the work I do is what I was born to do, God wants me to do. God is with me, and no great battle in life has ever been easy and without fear and setbacks. Pick up your sword and go slay those dragons, Lisa. My gut is telling me not to abandon this course.

8. **Action:** Give it time, but within the next four months, run another course.

One of the great tools I picked up from an interview guest, Brittany Hoopes,[1] was the mantra, "I can do hard things." Whenever I want to give up, I look back at my life and ask myself, "Is this harder than that last thing I got through?" If the answer is no, I grit my teeth and repeat: "I can do hard things, I can do hard things."

So much of our eleven million bits of subconscious identity comes from a small human's interpretation of the messages that The World Out There told them. It leaves Deep Grooves in our life where the weeds start to grow or our roots absorb faulty thinking. But if we just look at our behaviour—both what we do and what we don't do, despite how much we want it—and do the work with our journaling process, we can not only learn to see our assumptions and interpretations but also have the opportunity to rewrite them and lay down a new stack of thinking in which the strong trees and beautiful flowers of our life can grow.

The Reverse Thinking Stack

1. What causes me to feel like I do now?

Trigger

Earliest event

2. What's going on below the surface?

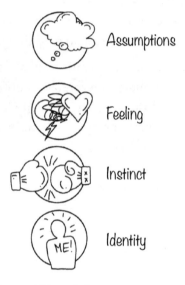

Assumptions

Feeling

Instinct

Identity

3. How can I do things differently?

Wisdom

Action

JOURNALING

What have you tried to change many, many times but haven't been able to? Go through the Reverse Thinking Stack (Trigger, Event, Assumption, Feeling, Instinct, Identity, Wisdom, and Action) and work out the Identity Statement you're believing, and what it needs to be to change your action.

Some ideas:

1. A pattern of responding to your spouse or kids or parents on an issue
2. Your eating or exercise regime
3. The new business you want to start or have tried starting a million times but have given up on
4. Sales calls that you need to make but haven't

Then, when you next find yourself angry, irritated, upset, hurt or feeling shame, take yourself through the Back-to-Back Thinking Stack—acknowledging first your real feelings in Thinking Stack One and then, when calm begins to set in, the story you need to be telling yourself and the actions you need to take in Thinking Stack Two.

If you want to see some of my Thinking Stacks on the issues I most struggle with in happiness, health, wealth, and work, go to www.LisaLinfield.com/DeepGroovesDownload and you can see behind the scenes how I use this.

6

Fitting In Versus Belonging

One of the biggest challenges of being human is this ancient brain believes that, for our own survival, we need to fit in and stay within our tribe.

Now, I do believe with all my heart that we are born to live in community with others and that we are better when we are in a relationship with all the people around us. And as much as I struggle to admit it, even the difficult people are necessary for our growth and development. They sharpen our skill set, challenge whether we truly live our values (it's easy to be nice to someone we like!), and make us appreciate how much we love those we choose to be with.

John laughs at me every time I've had a difficult client or a situation where I'm exposed to a difficult human or a rocky marriage. I always come bouncing in, sit almost on top of him on the couch, and tell him how wonderful he is and how much I love him. My marriage is in *no* way perfect, and I'm definitely *not* the most perfect wife or easiest person. But oh, my word, there are some marriages that would be my idea of hell and some very difficult people out there and it makes me appreciate greatly my wonderful husband and the marriage we have.

Money gives physical expression to what's going on inside a human and within our relationships and to our real values because they are expressed in the choices we make. When I work with people on their finances, I truly get to see behind the mask we all show The World Out There. I get to see the Real Reasons, the real people, the real state of financial affairs and marriages. But even these difficult interactions and difficult people sharpen my sword and build my appreciation for the amazing humans I do have in my life. My tribe. The people I like spending time with. The people I choose to walk with.

The other day I read a quote from Brené Brown that is one of the key concepts in her book *Braving the Wilderness*:

"Fitting in is the greatest barrier to belonging." [1]

Let's just sit with that a while.

The greatest barrier to feeling like you truly belong in life is trying to fit in.

I can't begin to tell you how much this has been playing on my mind—a theme of many lessons in the last few months. I am beginning to understand that I've spent my whole life trying to fit in—at work, at school, as an adult—when what I should have been doing was seeking out people and places where I truly belong.

Brené's summary is that belonging means showing and standing for our authentic self, while fitting in means acclimating or changing ourselves in response to the world around us.

I love this quote from her:

*"Belonging is the **innate human desire** to be part of something larger than us. Because this yearning is so primal, we often try to acquire it by fitting in and by seeking approval, which are not only hollow substitutes for belonging, but often barriers to it. Because true belonging only happens when we present our authentic, imperfect selves to the world, **our sense of belonging can never be greater than our level of self-acceptance.**"* [2]

The first thing that strikes me is that wanting to belong is an *innate human desire*. It exists in all of us, no matter how introverted or extroverted, how relational or non-relational we are. We all want to belong. It comes back to our survival being intrinsically linked to being within the protection of the tribe.

As an introvert who loves to recharge by herself, I find the public nature of the work I do tiring. Put that together with three little gorgeous humans, and my best day at work is a day in my office with nothing in my diary and just me and my computer and the ability to be creative and get things done. But, at the same time, starting my three businesses has been all-consuming over the last few years—and what's suffered is my social life. At a soul level, I deeply miss my friends, my tribe, those people I feel safe with, where I belong—and looking at those Facebook posts of friends having fun, I wish I'd been invited along.

The second thing I love is that Brené Brown recognises that we try actively to belong. That trying is called *fitting in*. When we try so hard, what we are actually doing is seeking approval for the version of ourselves we calculated and *created* to best match the tribe out there, not the version of ourselves we truly are.

Lastly, she gives us the answer to my question of "how do we belong?" from her research.

> *"True belonging only happens when we present our authentic, imperfect selves to the world."*

And that's the real crux. Being willing to present our imperfections when all we want so badly is to be perfect. It goes against what we've been told so often: be the good little girl. Wash your face, brush your hair—people are coming. Always show others how perfect you are and how perfect our family is—not the exhausted, irritable, dirt-caked version you were ten minutes ago.

These days this issue is exacerbated by Instagram, where the unspoken rule is to always show everyone the most perfect life you lead. One of the things I love about Mel Robbins is her mix of Instagram videos of her looking perfect, of her sweating, panda-eyed from mascara after gym, and of her with no makeup and hair in rollers as she sprouts forth her latest thought.

Joining a Group

I love the serendipity of life, the coincidences of God, and sometimes I just have to giggle at His sense of humour. At the time I was preparing and outlining this chapter, I was accepted into a small group of great financial advisers who meet to share knowledge and support each other. Now that I work by myself, the thing I miss most about corporate life (besides the pay check!) is being with like-minded humans, all working toward a common goal—the team factor. So being accepted into this network was a big deal for me in my quest to find humans with whom to share my professional journey.

That morning, as I was collecting my thoughts on fitting in versus belonging, I got added to the WhatsApp group. For two days I stayed silent, watching as birthday messages streamed in for people I didn't know yet.

And then my moment came—someone asked a technical question. Desperate to fit into a group who knew each other well and had been together for a long time, I pounced on the opportunity to prove I did in fact fit in, could contribute meaningfully, and wow them with my knowledge—all in an attempt to make sure they didn't regret their decision to let me join their tribe.

I hauled out my textbook, put together a fantastic synopsis (with citations of the relevant tax laws), and then proudly posted my response on the group, knowing that this would reassure them of my place as a value-adding member.

The minute my phone vibrated and I saw there was a message in the group, I couldn't wait to read it—the good little girl in me was so excited for the praise I was guaranteed to receive. Only the message said nothing of the sort. Gently and graciously, one of the ladies responded, and, to my horror, I discovered I'd made a stupid error, gone on a complete tangent, and my answer was wrong.

I wanted to crawl under my desk again.

Idiot. Fruitloop. Loser. Useless. What on earth were you thinking?

And then I giggled. And giggled, and giggled, and giggled.

I realised that I was trying so hard to fit in that I messed up. Instead of allowing the natural "getting to know you" process to unfold over time, I was so desperate to be found worthy of being included that in the process I'd made a complete idiot of myself. And now I was shaming myself into a massive downward spiral.

The Gorilla in the Room

It's enough. Like you, what I want most is to belong. I'm exhausted from trying for forty-four years to fit in.

> *"Our sense of belonging can never be greater than our level*
> *of self-acceptance."*

Ah, now there's the challenge. In that one little half sentence lies the biggest gorilla dancing in the room. I have to start with me—the real me—and I've got to belong in my own skin first. To accept that who I am is exactly who I was meant to be—and that that version is good enough—not the version The World Out There says I'm supposed to be. I need to let go of the little seeds of negativity and self-condemnation that I have planted and watered and nurtured my whole life, because they've grown into huge happiness-eating carnivorous weeds that have strangled my Best Life Tree and eaten my joy. It's enough.

I want a deep sense of belonging, not just a little glimpse of it every now and then. A deep, body-enveloping sense of belonging, to myself, to the people I interact with, to all humanity. Always. But how will I ever find that if I don't even feel comfortable in my own skin?

Jess and I were talking about girls at school who were comfortable in their own skins. There were two in particular she picked out. I asked her, "How do you know they are comfortable in their own skins?"

And she thought a while and answered, "I dunno. You just know."

We both thought a while and then I asked her, "If you 'just know' that someone else is comfortable in their own skin, do you think they 'just know' if you're not comfortable in your skin?"

After another pause, she answered, "I guess so."

And that's the challenge. We are so busy trying to put on a mask to fit in—yet as sentient beings, we know when someone is not truly comfortable in their own skin. Science has shown that our heart has an electromagnetic field 5,000 times greater than our brain. It's why you can "feel" someone staring at you or sense someone's unhappiness before they say a word. We perceive before we think.

Earlier this year I hosted Supper Club at my house. There are usually twelve of us, but this particular winter evening, there were only four. Just a nice, intimate dinner with yummy, warm food and great wine on a freezing night. We got onto chatting about this concept of feeling like you belong. I've been part of this group of vivacious women for fourteen years, so you'd think that by now I felt like I belonged! But I shared with them that for so many years in the beginning, I didn't feel like I belonged. I felt like the boring outsider looking in on this amazing, gorgeous group of vivacious women. The left foot in a right shoe. The piece of the puzzle in the puzzle box that doesn't actually fit but somehow got there from another puzzle.

But I also shared that it had *nothing* to do with them. It was all on me.

You see, my Supper Club has some of the most beautiful women God put on this earth. I remember my very first one, three of them had just been on the covers of magazines. I leant toward my friend who introduced me to the group and said, "The only magazine I'll ever be in is Forbes or Finance Week, and not for my beauty!" Not only were they beautiful, but to me when I first joined it felt like they led perfect thirty-something lives whilst I was just struggling to keep my head above water having just moved back to South Africa from London.

I didn't feel like I belonged because their beauty magnified my biggest insecurity, the part of me that has never fallen into that self-acceptance bucket: my physical looks—the ugly, fat, acne-filled teenager. And despite the fact that I'm married to the most gorgeous, tall, strong, blonde hunk of a man who thinks I'm the sexiest wife alive, I'm still stuck when it comes to being happy with my looks. Most days it doesn't bother me. But in the presence of beauty, I'm still that curled-up teenager, crying on her dormitory bed as her friends all went to the ball. This thinking, this earliest event, meant I couldn't accept that I would *ever* belong in a group of such beautiful women.

One of them asked if I felt like I belonged now—fourteen years later. Mostly, I do. But that's because I'm losing *my* belief that the entry criteria to belonging in the world (not just Supper Club) is that we have to be beautiful, perfect humans. It amazes me though, how quickly I can trigger back when I see a photo one of them posts on Facebook of us all—I see the ugly duckling hanging with these beautiful swans.

Starting my own business has forced me to seek my sense of self-worth from me, not the World Out There. My whole life I've sought that sense of worth from the praise of parents, teachers, professors, bosses, and colleagues telling me how great my work is. If my self-esteem was a nine out of ten at the peak of my corporate career, it's now a four. But it is the most rock-solid four because it comes from me and no-one can take that away by withholding praise. I've needed to learn to encourage, praise, and build *myself* up—because the pot plant on my desk isn't going to do it!

It was interesting that my friends at supper club had noticed it too. They also felt that I was more comfortable, happier, more settled in the last two years than I had been before. Somehow, Jess was right—we all feel the subtle shifts in a human when it comes to their own sense of self. We know who is comfortable in their own skins and who is not.

Isn't that such an irony? That we try so hard to fit in, to show the perfect mask outward, yet people around us sense deep in their souls whether we are being our authentic self or not. So we might as well work out how to be us, how to accept who we are, because we're not fooling anyone!

"How do you do that, Mamma?" Jess asked.

The Integrative Change Model

I love a good framework to help me learn or understand something. And one of my superpowers is integrative thinking—joining the dots between multiple different things. So here are four different models all synthesised into one framework to help us rethink this whole thing as to how we become more comfortable in our own skin. I call it the Integrative Change Model. If you want to download a printable copy for your journal to support your thinking, go to www.LisaLinfield.com/DeepGroovesDownload.

Integrative Change Model

The base of the model, the steps, comes from the Four Stages of Competence model.[3] Think of it as a bit like learning to ride a "big girl" bike. When we're young, riding our plastic scooter, we have no idea that we want to, need to, or could ride a "big girl" bike. We're blissfully unaware. This stage is called **Unconscious Incompetence**—we don't know that there's something out there that we have no idea how to do.

We then have this Ah-Ha moment (and there's a whole science behind those!) when we see the big girls ride their big girl bikes and think—"Hey, this little scooter is for the birds! I want to ride that big metal bike that goes so fast." We then jump on that bike, feeling invincible, pop our little feet on the peddles, and take off just like them— only to come crashing to the ground a few meters later. It's the first time we become aware that we don't actually know how to ride the bike, and we're going to have to learn. We become **Consciously Incompetent.**

So we get taught the theory from our mum and begin practicing, thinking deeply about every single move, reflecting with our mum why we fell this last time. It's the Active Learning Cycle we learnt earlier about in chapter two. Whilst we still think about how to ride the bike as we wobble down the road, we're **Consciously Competent.**

Only once we practice it a lot, fall a bit, and think some more do we build a habit of pedals, gears, steering, and flying. Within a few weeks, we don't even think about it—it's second nature to ramp over that hill. Now we're **Unconsciously Competent**. We're competent at riding the bike, and we do it without having to think about it—we go on instinct.

Learning anything as an adult follows that cycle, but when it comes to changing our behavioural and thinking habits, our unconscious beliefs have been so deeply ingrained in our subconscious that we unfortunately don't go quickly one way up that ladder to mastery. In real life, we spend a lot more time going up and down the learning curve. Moments of conscious competence lead to being unconsciously competent at times, only to find ourselves slipping back down and unconsciously trying to fit in the next time we feel insecure.

In order to work through the Integrative Change Model, I developed the Four Steps to Changing Your Behaviour. It's a simple framework you can print and stick in your journal (download it at www.LisaLinfield.com/DeepGroovesDownload) that will take you through the model that you can use to help you understand and change your behaviour. Whilst I've tailored it for fitting in, you can use it to work out how to behave differently when you're angered or irritated or frustrated.

Four Steps to Changing Your Behaviour

The first step of self-acceptance is non-judgemental observation— becoming conscious of when you're trying to fit in—having that Ah-Ha moment.

I'm a journeyer myself, so I can't say I've nailed this. As I said, just a few weeks ago, I messed this one up in spectacular fashion with my new network of financial advisers.

But what I've learnt is that it's a journey that starts with just "watching yourself" from above as you interact with others—it always starts with that step. The key, however, is *non-judgemental* observation. No beating yourself up. Just watch with love, empathy, humour, and kindness, as if you were watching your daughter. And listen to your body signs of shame or anxiety—for me, the elephant on my chest. This Ah-Ha moment when you realise you're fitting in can come in the moment, but many times it's so habitual we actually need to stop and consciously think about it, discovering it through journaling or a conversation with a friend.

I want to next-level my life. To live my Best Life I need to change my thinking. So I choose to speed up those Ah-Ha moments by including journaling into my morning routine. I take twenty minutes each day to journal-pray. As I said, I'm not very good at sitting with a clear mind and meditating or reflecting on my day, so I combine my prayers and journaling in the following routine (which you can download on www.LisaLinfield.com/DeepGroovesDownload to put in your journal):

1. **Give thanks**—gratitude is crucial to happiness and it's proven that you do your best thinking in the presence of gratitude. After I write down what I'm thankful for, I pause and "re-live" that feeling. I'll write down something like, "Thank you, Lord, for the laughter at supper last night," and then I'll close my eyes and take myself back to supper and hear the laughter of my children, looking down at all of us (me included) from the sky. Imagining *with* emotion has been a game changer—I've always done gratitude journaling (writing down a minimum of three things I'm grateful for each day) but introducing a pause to re-live the moment with all the emotion is far more effective in building deep gratitude and a higher level of happiness that can last the whole day than just writing down three things and moving on—and takes only ten seconds longer.

2. **Reflect** on yesterday—this forces that Active Learning Cycle for me.

- What went well—I scan my day quickly and force myself to bullet-journal my day's highlights: things I got done, great conversations, little micro-successes.
- What was a big Ah-Ha—something I learnt, a new perspective I gained, some insight that made me rethink a viewpoint, idea, or strategy.
- What would I do differently—this is when I look at where I've messed up and why. Sometimes this is straightforward, but sometimes this is when I would go into a Reverse Thinking Stack to try and find the real reason for my words, actions or thoughts. If I don't have time to think, I'll highlight it or put a star next to it to come back and explore it later—but I find just the action of kicking off a Reverse Thinking Stack means my brain starts searching for the answers in the background while I go about my day.
- When were you trying to fit in and why—this is a specific section of reflecting on things I would do differently. It's me forcing myself to be more aware of where I'm insecure and why.

3. **Intention**—then I set intentions for the day.

We all start in the state known as Unconscious Incompetence—we don't realise that we are trying to fit in as we've been doing it for so long. This was me when smashing off that know-it-all, trying-to-impress message on the WhatsApp group, so desperately trying to fit in. At this point, we're on autopilot, functioning on instinct—the wrong instinct—but the one we've built into a Deep Groove we just fall into. Our behaviour is driven by a deep identity belief—mine being that I'm not good enough to belong to this group of talented advisers. And because I'm not good enough, I compensated by using what The World Out There has told me is my strength—being clever.

We then have an Ah-Ha moment that shows us where we're going wrong—that moment we realise we're operating from the wrong instinct. Sometimes that comes from a book, from a conversation, from someone else's coaching and feedback, or from doing the work to listen to our gut or journal—like I try to every day. It always involves being mindful of our behaviour and being able to take ourselves out of the space of judgement and into the space of observer—of ourselves, those around us, the situation, and the reactions—both logical and emotional. This is the reflection phase.

My Ah-Ha moment, my trigger for reflection, was when the WhatsApp message came back that in fact, my long thesis was wrong, which caused me to reflect and I realise I had messed up because I was trying to fit in.

The second step is to work out why you're trying to fit in.

You can only begin changing what you're conscious of, and that's why the journaling process helps you identify the *what*—the symptom, the signpost, the weed above the surface, the dead branch on the tree. But you can only change your behaviour once you know the *why*. The Real Reason why, not the Good Reason we justify to ourselves. Why were you triggered in the first place? What about this other person or situation made you behave that way? You need to find the real answer—not the good answer you tell yourself—the one that resonates deep within your soul and gives you that Ah-Ha moment.

When I need to look deeply at times when I was trying to fit in, I always use a technique that I lovingly refer to as "Five Whiskeys and a Heineken." I have no idea when I first heard of it referred to as that, but it's a lovely "Suitcase Phrase" (more on this later) of a process of continuously questioning who, what, where, when, why (the five Whiskeys), and how (the Heineken), until you leave the land of Good Reasons and head into the land of Real Reasons. The Five Whiskeys and a Heineken reminds me that I need to go through at least six cycles of questioning in order to get to the real reason.

One of the biggest ways I try to fit in is by oversharing. When I do my Reverse Thinking Stack, and I force myself to keep pushing through my Five Whiskeys and a Heineken test, it's a combination of a huge insecurity around silences and a deep desire to fit in.

The silence insecurity originally comes from a specific incident in the morning carpool when I was a little person. That morning, everyone was quiet in the car, probably just waking up. Frustrated with the taxi-driver element of the morning lift club (I can now *so* relate), the dad dropping us at school commented that we all needed to learn the art of making conversation, that boring people sat in silence, and no one liked boring people. From that moment on, I've always held a huge anxiety about silence and the fear that people would think I was boring.

That message was reinforced as I grew up. My grandfather was a politician, and so my mum and her sisters were brought up with Dale Carnegie skills in making conversation with anyone, including the person on your right and left, and making sure you keep scanning the room to ensure that no one is left out. We were never children who were seen and not heard. My parents always made sure that we would join their dinner parties in the beginning to meet their friends, and we were expected to make conversation. "Fine," "Good," and "OK" were not acceptable answers. We were always expected to ask the other person how they were and be able to make conversation around their interests and work.

As I raise my children, I believe that the skill of making and contributing to conversation is one of *the* most important skills I can teach them, and I'm so grateful I was taught those skills.

But I do moderate that with the ability to feel comfortable in silences—a skill I've learnt from my introverted husband. As I've got older, I'm more conscious of *when* I'm trying to fill the silences and *why* I'm doing that. Is it out of respect for the other person and focussed on them, or am I oversharing out of my insecurity? Am I acting out of the anxiety of being thought of as boring or the desire to fit in (by short-circuiting the "get to know you" process so you'll instantly like me)? It always intrigues me as to why I want to do that—I don't have enough time to see my closest friends, so I'm definitely not looking to add more to my life!

But only by journaling, by digging deeper, do I even become conscious of when I'm doing it and why. Only once that happens can I begin to plan how to change my behaviour. The main thing is *not* to judge yourself in this process of observation. There is *never* great learning in the presence of judgement as your subconscious will shut you down for fear of Cruella hurting you. You have to just sit with the discomfort of observation, like you're watching a movie of yourself. The minute you start judging, you'll start defending. So just watch, just journal. And when you find yourself judging, have the grace to giggle at yourself.

The third step is to practice being you, by first planning what to do differently.

The next step in the adult learning model after becoming Consciously Incompetent is to become Consciously Competent. That means that you practice being you. This sounds so odd—if belonging is about being authentically you, isn't it a contradiction to have to practice being you?

The Active Learning Cycle says once you've reflected and concluded that you were trying to fit in, you plan how you would behave differently. My plan is that when I feel the urge to fit in, either by talking (or texting in my mess-up case!), that I purposefully stay quiet, which can mean sitting with the painful discomfort of silence. So when I feel the sensation in my body or recognise that I'm trying too hard to fit in, I know I need to consciously follow my chosen action, rather than respond unconsciously to the situation.

Shortly after the WhatsApp incident, I had my first informal knowledge-share lunch with the network. As I got ready that morning, I decided I was going to put on one of my snazzy work dresses—the power dress look—to make me feel like I was on top of the game. I was looking through my dresses, debating which one, when I caught myself and packed up, laughing. I was doing it *again*, and the pressure on my chest was sending me warning signs galore. I was trying to fit in instead of being me and belonging. So I closed the dress cupboard, opened my normal cupboard, and went as I usually would—comfortable trousers, top, and dress-up flip flops.

Aware of all these triggers, at the lunch I was conscious to keep quiet rather than fill the silence and to share only when I had something to contribute. I was effectively practicing being the real me and not the fit-in, over-talkative version.

But, as you can see, whenever we try to learn a new way of being, we tend to go up and down the ladder of consciousness and competence. Just when I had consciously caught myself on the WhatsApp, I unconsciously did it again with the dress. The World Out There's messages and our interpretation of them is so deeply ingrained that we find ourselves falling back into those old Deep Grooves of behaviour.

Whilst the challenge of Consciously Incompetent is not judging and being kind with yourself, the challenge of Consciously Competent is living with the awkwardness of the moment. Because you've been so practiced at fitting in, it now feels "natural," yet it's not authentic. So practicing authenticity feels unnatural.

The fourth step is to practice enough in different circumstances to make it an unconscious habit.

Charles Duhig's work on habits is brilliant.[4] The habit cycle always starts with a trigger, followed by a behaviour, then lastly, a reward. Identifying the triggers helps us know when we're about to do something we want to change.

The Habit Model

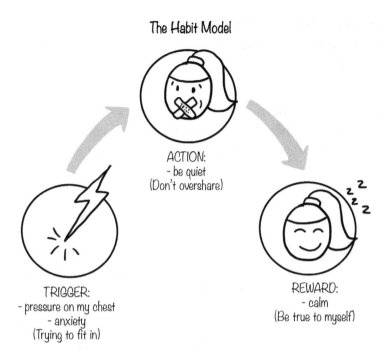

ACTION:
- be quiet
(Don't overshare)

TRIGGER:
- pressure on my chest
- anxiety
(Trying to fit in)

REWARD:
- calm
(Be true to myself)

For me, my biggest triggers for trying to fit in are new situations with new people, when I try too hard to get them to like me. This is particularly exaggerated when I perceive the person has a higher 'status' than I have—they're cleverer, more pretty, or more successful. Physically, I feel this trigger as pressure on my chest, the anxiety.

My plan for changing my behaviour or response to the trigger is to focus on being quiet when I want to overshare and tell you why you should like me, or prove to you that I'm worthy of playing in your league.

The reward is greater peacefulness. The feeling of calm in my soul of knowing that I feel comfortable in my own skin. That I'm not trying so hard to fit in, to justify that I'm worthy of your approval.

With enough practice, you will eventually become Unconsciously Competent. That means you are authentically you, unconsciously and effortlessly.

But one word of warning. I've found self-development to be like an onion. You become more or less unconsciously competent at one level, thinking that you've got this nailed, just to find that you're back at the beginning, discovering you're unconsciously incompetent at another deeper layer of the similar thing. This is a lifelong journey of growth and development.

Why does it take so much to energy to change daily micro habits? Because we've spent so long believing and behaving in line with what The World Out There says that finding our own path is like trying to climb out of a canyon sometimes. Doable? Yes. How? One step at a time.

JOURNALING

Download and print the 'Four Steps to Changing Your Behaviour' Framework from www.LisaLinfield.com/DeepGroovesDownload to stick into your journal and work through the following:

- Without judgement or criticism, where are you trying to fit in instead of being you and allowing yourself to belong?
- Why is that? What's the trigger? Practice the Five Whiskeys and a Heineken structure of continuously asking in order to work out the real reason, rather than the good reason. Use the Reverse Thinking Stack to work out the Real Reasons if it helps.
- Summarise your action plan as to what you need to do differently when that trigger arises.
- Seek out opportunities to practice it, trying to make it a habit.

Then, try at least three to five times a week to do the 20 Minute Morning Routine of journaling to build a practice of gratitude, reflecting on your day (Active Learning Cycle), and scanning your day for any times when you were trying to fit in. Download it at www.LisaLinfield .com/DeepGroovesDownload.

7

The Groove

I'm a person who thinks in pictures. I guess that's why I love frameworks that help me sort complex information into a simple picture form.

Imagine a huge, green field with beautiful stream winding through it. It's a little stream, so it just makes a little dent in the field. But over time as the rain comes and more water flows from it, it starts to make a groove, a river bed, deeper in the field. As many years pass, and more water flows, and the floods come, that river bed starts to become a deep cut through the field and rocks that becomes a valley, allowing even more water to tumble down into the river, which is now filled with strong currents as the water rushes past. And over centuries, it becomes a canyon—as the water cuts a majestic pathway through the rocks.

Like the way the river carves a Deep Groove the water will habitually flow through, so the many different voices of The World Out There, together with our personal experiences, assumptions, and interpretations, become the groove we fall into in life. When we first start doing something, we will look to our parents, our friends, Google or social media to find out how to do it. When that seems to work, or we don't get kicked out of the tribe, it becomes ingrained as a habit—an automatic way of doing something.

The Groove of Corporate Culture

One great example of grooves is company culture. Watch new people join a company—it's always interesting to see how quickly they are able to suss out who's who; what's acceptable to wear, say, and do; and how quickly they fall into the groove of the company culture. To counter this, one of my previous bosses, Clive, had a great practice for newcomers. For our first three months, he asked us to journal all the different things we would change about the organisation.

You see, each of us comes from a context of another company or culture. When we first arrive in the new company, the differences in "the way things are done around here" are so striking, it almost smacks us in the face. The glaring omissions in value propositions, processes, and people seem so obvious. Over the full three-month period, a new person has enough time to see a fuller view of the less obvious, more subtle elements of culture and informal power structures that wield the most power in the company. But it is short enough that you haven't yet become absorbed fully into the culture.

He then challenged us to look at those reflections on the anniversary of our joining for every year after that. Why? Because when we first arrive, we're like a pink dot in a purple sea. But over time, we take on enough purple on the outside to fit into the corporate tribe, into the groove.

Soon we lose that sense of shock at "the way things are done around here" and become part of the structures that first tolerate and then perpetuate those very ways. As we go with the flow of the river, we fall slowly, gently, but surely into the groove, and as it becomes deeper in our lives, it becomes far harder to climb out of and far safer to stay there. The groove becomes our comfort zone. And pretty soon we become a purple dot in a purple sea, with the glimmers of pink becoming less and less frequent.

It's how our ancient brain is wired—to fit into the tribe. Those who survived ice ages and droughts were those who could adapt, work together, and fit in. The very fact that we sit here today means that we've descended from the adaptors and adaptation in each of us is a strong genetic survival instinct.

The wonderful sophistication of us humans is the ability to sense and integrate all the millions of little data points that make up the company culture—conversations, dress, position at tables, body language, and unsaid words—to quickly identify how to walk, live, exist, and even thrive in the groove. Arrive at work once in a suit when everyone else is in jeans, and you'll never be in a suit again. No one needs to tell you. Watch someone else talk when the iron-fist boss wants to hold court and they're silently killed with an evil glare, and you'll learn quickly when you speak and when you don't.

From our internal perspective, we just feel ourselves becoming more "at home," feeling less different, and blending in with the purple people. But the process of blending in requires us to effectively zoom in, and we slowly lose sight of the company culture from the big-picture perspective we first had when we left our old company and came to this new one. We begin to believe that this is the way "things are done around here." We believe the stories that others did try to change it and fail, so there must be no other way.

But when we do take the time to zoom out, or reflect, we realise that our little pink dot is now marching in the same direction as everyone else, in the path The World Out There tells us is right—for them, for us, for our life. We see we have lost a piece of ourselves, of who we are, our voice has become quieter as we speak in the voice of the company tribe.

But, we can challenge ourselves to see the current context within *our* bigger picture of our Best Life. Do we really want to be that grumpy person who believes nothing can be changed, that we are powerless, and that we just have to accept this bully boss?

The Groove of Family

One of the deepest grooves we experience first in life is family.

Every family tribe has a groove—ways of speaking, different ideas on what makes good manners, hierarchy, when to be quiet, acceptable jokes, informal alliances. These grooves of the way our family works, who our family is, even "right and wrongs" develop over many years, even passing down over generations. And given that the two people in a marriage always come from two different families with their different grooves, it's surprising that any marriage ever lasts!

When you first introduce your boyfriend or girlfriend to the family, they're on best behaviour, trying to suss out what those grooves are, creep gently into the larger family groove, and make sure they don't step on anyone's toes.

Over time as the dating progresses, they slowly make space for themselves in the groove, working out the rhythm, figuring out which fights are worth it and which aren't. They start building their own alliances with family members they are more comfortable with, those they sense have their back.

The engagement and wedding period then introduces a whole new stressful set of dynamics, when everyone does the groove dance in a concentrated period of time. Long-held issues surface inside the family, money dynamics rear their head, the integration of the in-law family accelerates, and the hierarchy goes through a huge shuffle. After all, whose wedding is it anyway?

And then, as those precious children start appearing, an entirely new groove shuffle begins. Norms on parenting start to get questioned, manners and "boundaries" become more hotly debated than world peace (relegating them to join religion, politics, and other "banned" family topics), and the hierarchy shuffles another space to the right, making space for the poppet, and slowly things settle again.

When I was twenty-five, I left the Deep Grooves of my life in Johannesburg and went to live in London. My time there was one of the best periods in my life—hard, but deeply transformational. I was taken out of every single groove of South Africa. The UK culture was different. I knew very few people, had one aunt and no other family, and no one knew a thing about me. They had no idea who my family was, whether my school was public or private, whether my university was good or bad, or whether my previous employer was a whale or sardine of industry.

That clean slate was liberating. Exhilarating.

I felt so free. My success was mine. My failure was mine. My experiences were mine. I could be who I wanted to be. I could discover and be me. Through those six years, I found my sparkle, my energy, my passion, my creativity. I made my own money, bought my own flat by myself, stood on my own feet.

Through finding my separateness, I felt excited at the end of the six years to go back home and feel a part of something again. A familiar culture, a family I adored, a life that felt comfortable.

I left South Africa a young single girl who had no clue who she was and returned a married woman. To say my re-entry into South Africa and my family was a crash course in grooves is an understatement. Coming back was like that frog being thrown right into hot water. My natural instinct (which I see frequently in people returning home or new daughters- and sons-in-law joining a family) was to jump out, find new friends, spend less time with my family.

There had been no gentle shuffle to accommodate my husband or the new me, no time for the hierarchy to shift one place to the right. And the spaces I had occupied had become filled with other friends and new dynamics. It was so hard fitting back into my family, my friends, and my life. I felt again like a pink dot in a purple sea.

Knowing how difficult this assimilation was for me, I can't help but wonder how blended families ever work anywhere in the world. Each member of the new couple and their kids have settled into their own groove in the post-divorce or post-death phase.

But, when the new couple gets married, not only are you trying to blend those two families' grooves together, and shuffle the hierarchies to the right with their exes, but you're also putting that chaos into the grooves of the broader family tribe without the benefit of time and shared history. The "babies" are sixteen, twelve, and eight, the parenting "norms" aren't even shared norms to the new couple let alone the broader family, and the unspoken expectations of the roles of "steps" become a source of friction, since no one knows what they're expected to do.

It makes me run and jump on the couch, hide under John's arm, and tell him how much I love him and how hard we need to work to stay together. That blended family thing is hard, so very, very hard. No matter how nice each of you are separately and how you are together as a new couple, the minute you put children, exes (who themselves have remarried), and broader families all together, you have chaos.

The Belonging in Deep Grooves

As much as we may fight against Deep Grooves when we find ourselves at odds with them, they also can be places where we find deep belonging. I realised this at my twenty-fifth school reunion. The previous reunions had been weighed down by an insecurity that we were all supposed to be showing each other how we were living these wonderful lives we dreamt about at school. But the twenty-fifth was different. Life had knocked every one of us, as it does, and with that—and age—came a sense of acceptance that the life we had was the one we were stuck with, and the need to show each other how wonderful our lives were had gone.

Most interesting was what was left without the pretences: a Deep Groove of people who had lived together and cared for each other at boarding school for five years. What was precious and unique about this groove was that it felt warm and accepting—and it encouraged and built you up. You see, we all knew each other before life's knocks had hit. And despite being teenagers trying so desperately to fit in with each other, when you live together for every minute of the day, you also intuitively know who the real person is despite the teenage crap and accept them for that. That teenage crap now gone, each person then felt even more the real person you knew and loved.

What was wonderful was being secure enough in that love to be able to laugh at life's knocks, to see the humour in the gap between The World Out There's picket fence, two and a half kids, and the golden retriever we all thought we would have and the curve balls life had thrown us. To see those who, despite life's knocks, had stepped into their voice, their unique talents, and had taken the lemons of life and made lemonade.

What was heart-breaking was to see how much of the optimism, hope, and inner sparkle had been knocked off some of the most wonderful, talented human beings. How the gap between that picket fence and their reality left a sadness that had stolen their joy and hope. With a few, there was almost a sense of giving up—that this is clearly how it was going to be, so they had resigned themselves to zooming in to that purple life. I wanted to hold them tight and remind them how talented, amazing, and unique they were, and how they needed to fight to get back in touch with the human they were created to be, before life's knocks.

The Challenge of Deep Grooves

It's made me wonder how many of us miss our true callings, our true greatness, our Best Life because we believe so deeply what The World Out There says happiness is. We believe there's some kind of schedule and that if we miss that train, there is no other, so we resign ourselves to the fact that we're in the bottom lane of The World Out There, and that's where we should stay.

It comes back to the challenge of the primitive part of our brain— that each time life knocks us, our brain shouts so loudly, "See, I told you so. The World Out There told you not to do it, to stay safe. And you didn't. And now it hurts. GET BACK INTO THE SAFE ZONE!" And we do. We sheepishly go back to serving the Master of Safety and The World Out There, with Cruella de Vil just screaming awful lashings in our heads.

But now, as we look back, there's this sense of loss, a sense that this path we're on—the groove we've found ourselves in—is not the road we could be on, that there's a gap between our potential and our reality. Where could we have been if we were braver, if we'd just picked ourselves up, dusted ourselves off, and risen like the phoenix from the ashes?

There's a song I love—one of those songs that fills your tummy and lifts your soul—that I'll often sing at the top of my voice, completely out of tune, as I hurtle down the highway. It's called "Tell Your Heart to Beat Again," and it's written by Matthew West, Bernie Herms, and Randy Phillips and most recently sung by Danny Gokey.

> *You're shattered*
> *Like you've never been before,*
> *The life you knew*
> *In a thousand pieces on the floor*
> *And words fall short in times like these*
> *When this world drives you to your knees*
> **You think you're never gonna get back**
> **To the you that used to be.**
>
> *Beginning*
> *Just let that word wash over you,*
> *It's alright now*
> *Love's healing hands have pulled you through*
> *So get back up, take step one*
> **Leave the darkness, feel the sun**
> **'Cause your story's far from over**
> **And your journey's just begun.**
>
> *Tell your heart to beat again*
> *Close your eyes and breathe it in*
> *Let the shadows fall away*
> *Step into the light of grace*
> **Yesterday's a closing door**
> **You don't live there anymore**
> **Say goodbye to where you've been**
> **And tell your heart to beat again.**[1]

What if that gap in your soul is your heart's way of telling you that you were made for so much more? That this groove you're stuck in is just a speck in the hills of opportunity, that there's another path? That there's still time for you to close the door on yesterday, to tell The World

80

Out There to back off, and for you to take off the heavy yoke of expectation and disappointment, so you can dance freely, stepping into the lightness of grace and the sunshine of love?

JOURNALING

- Is there a part of your life where you feel like this is as good as it gets? Your work, relationship, wealth or health? Using 5 Whiskeys and a Heineken and the Reverse Thinking Stack Framework, work out what you're believing and why.
- Over the next week, watch yourself in each of your different grooves, and journal your grooves, the unwritten behaviours, the no-go topics. Then, over time, work out what underpins them and whether you think that it works for you.

8

The Gap

The body has approximately 37.2 trillion cells in it, and each cell has its own little brain called DNA that tells it what type of cell it needs to be and how to keep surviving, repairing, and thriving. The same DNA code knows how to tell an eye cell to be an eye, a lung cell to be a lung, and a thumb cell to be a thumb. Each one contains three billion base pairs of building blocks which, when stretched out, is approximately three meters long. Its amazing structure enables it to curl up into just six microns, or six one-millionths of a meter. If you were to stretch out all the DNA in your body back to back, it would go twice around the solar system. Yet it occupies less than a speck on the planet.

After attending medical school and studying the body in detail, and now knowing that the body of medical knowledge doubles every seventy-two days, I have come to believe that this body of mine is no accident. Every human is a miracle, and the structure of every plant, bird, and blade of grass is a phenomenal work of creativity and genius—not one an accident. Each of us was perfectly created with *both* our strengths and weaknesses for our particular path in life. We were lovingly designed for our unique purpose, to support, lead, and further the humans around us.

You are no accident.

So it's no wonder that most of us feel a gap in our soul. You see, the path that The World Out There has told us we should follow is not our unique path but a bad mix of parts of others' paths. And the deeper we subscribe to that path, the further away we get from our personal best path designed for our unique blend of strengths and weaknesses. And the gap that it creates becomes the hole in our soul.

The Gap

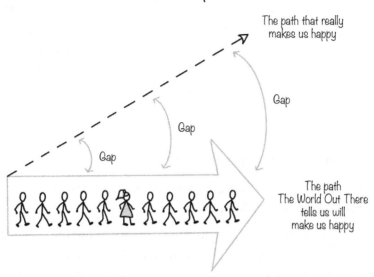

Each of us (unless we are a narcissist) lives with our worst, most brutal critic. Our inner Cruella de Vil, unless kept in check, loves using The World Out There's chants to beat us up and point to our failures.

- You see, you're not as wealthy as the others.
- Your career is not as successful as everyone else's.
- Even if you are CEO, you must be doing something wrong because The World Out There told you it would feel like you were king of the castle, and all it feels like is everyone's crap lands on you.
- Your body is not as thin as everyone else's.
- Your children are not as perfect because you're terrible at parenting.

And on and on it goes.

But what if we're trying so hard to fit what The World Out There tells us that we miss the amazing, far happier, far more fulfilling path we're supposed to be on?

What if we shut up Cruella and rather listened and acted upon The Still Small Voice? You know, the one that whispers that no matter what The World Out There tells us we should be doing, we know we're stuck in a groove that's not our unique path? That voice tells us that selling out our souls, our passions, and our values to keep up with The World Out There is only going to lead us to a place of loneliness. That spending time in a job or with people that make us feel insecure and unloved is never going to make us happy. That striving to be a person who we were never meant to be is not good for us.

Our Unique Innate Greatness

What if our soul knows how great we could be, how high we could soar, and how happy we were born to be?

What if we fear our greatness because we know the journey to reach it *is* a journey of stumbling and falling? Of fighting and slaying dragons, of going against the short-term hits of happiness from The World Out There. We're afraid of venturing into other tribe's lands, meeting unknown terrains and conditions that will scare us. What if we are scared our greatness will take us outside the tribe so we'll no longer fit in? That if we achieve that greatness, other tribes will try and steal that from us, pull us down so they'll be the top of the totem pole?

One of my favourite quotes is by Marianne Williamson:

> "*Our deepest fear is not that we are inadequate. Our deepest fear is that we are powerful beyond measure. It is our light, not our darkness that most frightens us. We ask ourselves, Who am I to be brilliant, gorgeous, talented, and fabulous? Actually, who are you not to be? You are a child of God. Your playing small does not serve the world. There is nothing enlightened about shrinking so that other people will not feel insecure around you. We are all meant to shine, as children do. We were born to make manifest the glory of God that is within us. It is not just in some of us; it is in everyone and as we let our own light shine, we unconsciously give others permission to do the same. As we are liberated from our own fear, our presence automatically liberates others.*"[1]

What if Marianne Williamson is right—what if the tribal instinct in us fears that we are "powerful beyond measure"? That we fear when we fall, our tribe will laugh at us for trying to find new territory of greatness?

As a people-pleaser, I deeply fear stepping outside the crowd. As a clutz with my spoken words, I'm guaranteed to say something that will result in me being ostracised from the crowd. But I also know that I will never, ever reach my goal of teaching one million women without stepping out of the tribe. No great change agent ever has. The heroes were *all* ostracised at some point.

God made every single one of us to shine, to add value, to walk a unique path. And I believe that without using our gifts to serve others, we will never truly find that path, nor our unlimited source of energy that comes from working in our passion and purpose.

I was born to be a princess warrior. I love that sense of doing the right thing, of the cause, the battle that's worth fighting for. When I worked in corporate, there were many times I felt that energy that came from a mission that used my skills and training perfectly for a specific job. But it was never sustainable, because sooner or later there'd be a new CEO or new management who would decide that the particular mission the previous boss gave me was not so critical, that what my team and I believed was right was actually wrong. With an ever-flip-flopping sense of right and wrong, my work over time became much less a source of passion and became just me using my skillset to do what I was asked to do.

The challenge that I faced was that I always thought that I was born to be a corporate girl. I loved working in corporate—they have big problems, big challenges, big complex puzzles that I could solve. I never saw myself as an entrepreneur. I felt safe to get that monthly pay check, and I loved having a boss I could please and a team I could belong to. To a certain degree I was so stuck in the corporate groove, I could never zoom out and see the possibilities of myself as an entrepreneur.

But I was just one semester into my B.Com Honours in Financial Planning when I felt the flame of a passion begin to burn again—it was smaller and more guarded in its optimism, but it was strong and unquenchable. Each lesson that I went through gave me a new insight that I could share with someone else: a friend going through a divorce, a single mum I knew, my father retiring, or John and I in our own personal investments.

By the time I finished my degree, became a board Certified Financial Planner® (CFP®), and set up my business, my vision was crystal clear: I wanted to follow the long lineage of amazing women in my family and work for the freedom of women in my time, in my generation. I wanted to fight for women's financial freedom, to break the centuries' old curse of women being completely reliant upon a man for financial support—and not just in South Africa. For women around the world.

Good, Great, and Hum

Every one of us can be good at anything. With enough work, a good teacher, perseverance, and determination, we can become good over time. But to be great, we need to have a passion for it. We need to have a love for what we are doing and work to our natural strengths. The real magic comes when we work in our purpose. Purpose is when we use our talents, hard work, and passion in the service of others. That's when we Hum.

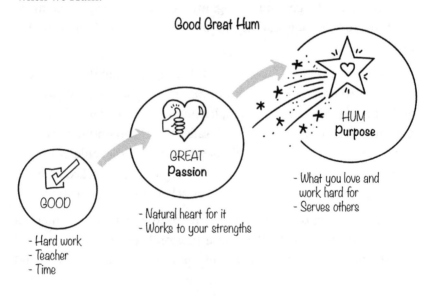

It's just how we were made as humans. We are designed to serve others with our passions—because the sum of all our talents means the whole tribe benefits. It's perfect in its design—somehow, working for an other-centred goal both pushes us further than we would for ourselves *and* moves the greater tribe forward. Working in our passion and purpose has an additional bonus of providing the energy we need to achieve it.

Ancient wisdom echoes this in every faith around the world, over centuries of records. I love this saying from 1 Peter 4:10 that re-enforces what Marianne Williamson says: "Each of you should use whatever gift you have received to serve others, as faithful stewards of God's grace in its various forms." Using your gifts to serve others is faithfully allowing God's grace to shine. Or, as Marianne says,

> *"We were born to make manifest the glory of God that is within us. It is not just in some of us; it is in everyone."*

Whether it's our inner fears, the storms we've weathered through life, or that we are so far stuck in our groove, we find ourselves going through the motions in parts of our life. "It's just the way it is," we tell ourselves. But somewhere deep in us we sense that we were made for more, and our soul prods us, "Is this all there is to life?" as it tries to highlight the gap between our unique purpose and the Deep Groove in which we're stuck.

Finding your purpose isn't always easy. But it does have a strange, never-ending energy cycle that keeps you moving on your unique path.

As much as I am passionate about what I do—and I am unwavering in my sense of purpose—there are weeks when I just want to throw the towel in, to drown my sorrows in a gin and tonic, and take away this big burden I've put on myself.

I remember one week that was filled with really difficult conversations with people who did not have enough money for retirement and who were really upset about the news that I was delivering. And whilst I knew that they didn't get cross with me personally, they did vent their anger and their frustration and their fears. They shot the messenger.

It also happened to be International Women's Week that week, and a company in England was running a campaign where women in their business stood with a sign that said a woman's name whom they admired and why they admired them. These signs spoke of amazing women. There was Sheryl Sandberg, Maya Angelou, someone's mother—people who had made a huge difference to these women's lives. And then in the bottom right-hand corner, one of the signs said Lisa Linfield.

Even as I write it now, I've got goose bumps all over me. The person in the picture said the woman they admired most was me—because I'd set a goal of teaching a million women about money and that they happened to be one of the first I taught. Robyn was one of my employees a few years ago in South Africa when I first started to try out what HumanSpeak was and how I could use it to teach investing and money management in a language normal humans would understand—no maths, no jargon. In a week where I wanted to throw in the towel, I saw that ad and burst into tears.

It was one of those days when the circle of energy had come back to motivate me. I realized that there *is* perpetual energy that can pick you up from absolute rock bottom and take you to a place where you can get on your way, shake off the dust, and keep on fighting.

Taking the Step

When I left the Deep Groove of corporate on my journey to find my unique path, my original business plan was for a wealth management business only. That was the first big step I had to make. There was no *Working Women's Wealth*, no podcasts, blog posts, or online teaching courses in my plan. I was going to teach women one by one in my wealth management business.

But as I walked that path, I felt my soul point out The Gap again. Whilst I loved the intellectual stimulation of working one on one with people to live their best lives, there was more I could do, there was a world of women I would never reach if I stuck to one on one. When I set the big, hairy, audacious goal of teaching a million women—that aligned with my passion and purpose—it forced me to find big step-change ways to reach it, to yet again take another step outside the groove of traditional financial advisers.

But the little-known secret about finding your unique path and big goals is that they require you *only* to take that first step, that first leap of faith in each fork in your path. That first step, however, is the hardest, since it's the one surrounded by fear, the one that takes you away from the safety of the groove and takes every ounce of courage just to step. But as you do so, the muddiness of uncertainty seems to part over time and that path becomes clearer to you.

My first step for *Working Women's Wealth* was my podcast. I can't begin to tell you how every fear I've ever felt came rushing all over me. Would anyone listen? What if I said things wrong? What if I was a terrible interviewer? My imposter syndrome was going through the roof. But I felt so strongly that if I had to teach all these people, I had no other way to get my message out there. I had no foot in the door with radio, no one who knew who I was or followed me. I figured podcasting was something new that I could build by myself. So, with absolutely no clue how to do it, I learnt and then started this podcast.

Whenever you're brave enough to take that first scary step, the rest seems to come.

I started to include videos and blog posts in my teaching, which soon evolved into keynote speaking and teaching companies and presenting at women's events about money. As each step of the journey progressed, that business plan I first created became further and further and further away.

When you first step out your groove of safety, your passion and purpose is just a tiny little flame of optimism with a huge dose of unknowns. But every time you honour that little flame, and step further into your purpose, it then starts to grow into a powerful fuel for the warrior in each of us.

That energy comes from not only having a passion for something but a passion that serves other people. And that's where your path will *always* be at odds to The World Out There's path. Why? Because The

World Out There tells you that you need to serve yourself first, make yourself great, win at all costs, become rich at the expense of others, and climb the ladder by treading on others.

When we follow the path of The World Out There, when we spend our time, money, and energy on trying to achieve its definition of happiness, we go against everything we were created to be.

We were created to be unique, not the cookie-cutter copies Instagram says we should be.

- We were created to have different talents, gifts, and passions—none better or worse than the next—and not to conform to all becoming lawyers, accountants, doctors, or nurses.
- We were created to live in community and use our passions to serve others by fulfilling our purpose—not to live totally individualistic lives profiting at the expense of others.
- We were created to manifest the glory of God within each one of us—not to manifest the selfishness of conformity.

Only when we honour each of these elements will we hum. We must find the energy within us to take the first step, but thereafter it will miraculously lift us up and keep us going when we want to throw in the towel.

But how do we find our passion and our purpose? It all starts with recognising the gap in our soul, which can be tricky. Sometimes, when I struggle to articulate what my gap is, I actually write to myself in the third person. I effectively employ debating or acting techniques by immersing myself as the protagonist. It starts off slow and jolting at first, but then amazingly, it seems to just pour out.

This is an example of how I start:

Dear Lisa,

- This is your (soul, guardian angel, guiding spirit, better half—whatever you want to call it). I am the part that loves you with everything I have, and I want to protect you and help you to live your Best Life. I've been watching you for a while now

in the area of (work, relationships, wealth, health) and I see (play back the video of what you see in great detail).
- This makes me feel (describe how what your better you sees makes you feel).
- I sense a better way might be . . .

Make sense? When I was leaving corporate, a summarised version looked as follows:

I see how tired and drained you are emotionally (let alone physically) from this corporate world. How weary you are from having your career determined by the shifting deck chairs in the layers above, by promises not kept, and by corporate restructures you can do little about.

I see how sad you are to miss the events at school that are so important to your little girls. How guilty you feel when you miss work to see them, and how much you crave the flexibility to choose where to spend your time.

*I see your disappointment, hurt, and frustration that you **know** you could be so much more, achieve more, contribute more to this world. And that gap between your potential and your current state in corporate is gnawing at your soul.*

*I sense a better way may exist. A path that enables you to control your destiny, where what you put in will generate results you desire. Where your success is yours, and your failures are yours too. A path that enables you not only to use your skills and talents but also to serve others. A happy path, a light path, a freer path. A path with the flexibility to be successful **both** as a mum and in your work.*

JOURNALING

Where does your soul prompt you that things aren't quite right? If needed, write a letter to yourself. You may also need to do a Five Whiskeys and a Heineken to dig deep into what the real reasons are you're feeling The Gap.

Signposts to Your Best Life

9

Listening to Your Gut:
The Guiding Signposts

Walid Azami was born in Kabul, Afghanistan—as you can imagine, a challenging place to grow up when there's been a war there for most of his life. He escaped the war as a young boy to live in America with his immigrant parents. I'd never heard of Walid or his story until I listened to Azul Terronez interview him on his podcast, Authors Who Lead. Walid was talking about how he dropped out of college to join the entertainment industry—and over time became a photographer to the likes of Kanye West, Jennifer Lopez, Usher, Ricky Martin, Maria Carey and Madonna, to name a few.

It's a fantastic interview with so many profound insights. Apart from Walid's unbelievable work ethic and stubborn determination in the face of poverty, what really struck me was how pivotal listening to his "sixth sense" was in being prepared for his "miraculous" opportunity that opened the door to celebrity photography. Maybe it strikes me because I wish I knew how to listen to my sixth sense more.

He talked about his watershed meeting with Jamie King, his mentor and a creative director, who told him that he was too worried about his ego—what people think of him—and not tuned in enough to himself or his greater calling. Walid protested, as most of us would. Jamie went on to explain:

> "The closest you'll ever be to God—or the Energy or the Light or the Universe or Mother Nature, or whatever you want to call it—is when you listen to your sixth sense. That's your gut instinct, your gut feeling, whatever you want to call it—that intuition. . . .

We are the only living creatures on earth that teach our children to shut that down. . . . If you want to do something, and if it's the craziest idea, then do it. If you want to get into a car, and something tells you, 'Don't get in this car right now, pull out.' Listen. Because you just got a direct phone call from God, or the Universe, or Energy or whatever you call it saying, 'This is not for your higher good, get out of this car now.'"[1]

He began to practice listening to his instinct—even when it seemed completely random and un-related to his current context—and that opened the door for the most out-the-blue opportunity to become Kanye West's personal photographer.

"The closest you'll ever be to God is when you listen to your sixth sense. . . . That instinct is a direct phone call from God."

How amazing is that?

I love his acknowledgement that The World Out There trains us from childhood *not* to listen to our gut or instinct, to shut it down in favour of logic and staying safely in the groove. Yet we are all created with this amazing way to communicate with God, with the greater Wisdom, and to see the signposts—using your gifts of logic, learning, *and* your gift of intuition, of sixth sense, of a phone call with God.

What if that empty feeling is God's way of showing you that you're on the wrong path? That the gap between you and The World Out There is not something to beat yourself up about but a signpost to the future life God wants you to have? The Wisdom of the Universe knowing you have so much more to give *and* to receive?

There are countless stories of people leaving high-paying jobs as bankers, lawyers, doctors to follow their heart to use their gifts and passions to serve others. So many of them talk about how everyone thought they were mad to give up the huge salary. That even though the beginning was tough—living off savings, not earning much, having no status—they felt an energy they hadn't felt in years. And over time, they went on to make more money than ever before, with more freedom, more passion, and more happiness.

Yes, there are those who took the leap and it never worked out. That's where the struggle that most people have comes into play. How do I know what's really Wisdom, and what's wishful thinking—or conversely, my negativity?

Starting Small

Like with everything, my advice is to start small. It's how I do it.

The first place I started with acting on God's phone calls was a little baby text message and now WhatsApp. You see, people come into my mind, sometimes in a happy way, sometimes because I have a sense I need to reach out and send them love. So when that happens, I send them a message.

The more I listened and acted, the more times people would say, "Wow, how did you know?" I can't begin to tell you how many times people have told me they just burst into tears when receiving my message—because they have been deeply struggling with something. Most times I'll then tell them that it's just God's way of telling them He knows they are in pain and that He loves them. At which point they just crumble, relieved to know *someone* sees their pain.

It's not always hard things. Sometimes it's practical. The other day I had a sense to message a friend I hadn't chatted to in a while. She shared with me that her helper was sick, her husband was away, and she felt they were drowning in laundry—she's a celebrity fitness person who goes through many gym outfits a day. It just happened that my ironing lady and cleaner had a spare Friday, and so I dropped her off that week to help my friend out.

But I've learnt to always message.

In my commitment to listen more to my intuition, I'm starting to learn how it manifests in my body. I mentioned that my shame feels like an elephant sitting on my chest bone. But my intuition, on the other hand, is a feeling I get in my head, like a thought knocking, knocking, knocking until I answer it. And some intuitions about direction, things I need to do, I feel in my tummy. Decisions about money, I'm learning, I feel in my heart, like an open door.

I am *totally* a novice at this—I guess it's the resistance of a highly analytical and logical person to venturing into the warm and fuzzies. In this field, you could say I'm a slow learner, but I keep at it because the more I honour it, the more things happen that validate not everything in the world is neat and tidy and fits into a logic box.

The Gut Calendar

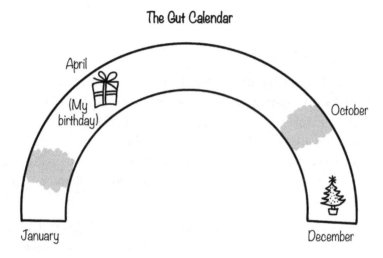

April

(My birthday)

October

January

December

Many times I sense things in pictures, especially when it comes to timing. I see a half circle calendar of the year and a darkness where it is on the calendar.

Just last week I was dropping off my daughter for orchestra practice at 6:30 a.m. On the way there, I passed two large SUV trucks parked nose to nose as they tried to jump-start a flat battery. I had a sense that I should pull over and offer to give them my extra-fat jumper cables we had at home for our SUV. But I drove past and dropped her off.

Usually, I'd head out the school gate and drive to my gym trainer session that starts at 7:00 a.m. But because I was trying to act on my instincts more, I decided to head back the way I came and stop to offer the cables. As it turns out, they had managed to get it started but were desperately keen to learn where I'd got those extra fat cables—since little cars and little cables struggle to jump start big ones.

Was my intuition wrong because they didn't need me to help them jump-start? On face value, yes. But maybe they needed the prompt to get the big cables because they were about to get stuck in a random place and the only nearby car would be a little one. Regardless, it took two minutes, I was proud of myself for listening to my intuition, and I'd lost nothing by doing it—and maybe even restored their sense that someone in humanity cares.

Pushing Through

The other thing I often find is that there is synchronicity in intuition. I may start with a sense that I've got to do something but it's not strong enough to actually act on it. When I start listening and ask God to open my heart to what I need to know, I'll find synchronicity in news stories, conversations with friends, out-of-nowhere interactions with old friends I hadn't seen in ages or total strangers—all pointing to the same lesson.

When it's a hard lesson or a deep lesson, and I'm fighting it, I almost feel like I butt up against resistance, which I've got to push through. For many of my nineteen years in financial services in corporate and the first two years on my own, I spoke very little about my time as a physical therapist (or 'physio' in South Africa). The good reason is that it wasn't relevant. The real reason is that I felt if I ignored that part of me and let the sleeping dog lie, people wouldn't know I was a physical therapist or that my undergraduate degree wasn't in business or accounting. They wouldn't have a reason to think less of me.

A similar theme happened when I started my financial planning business. I would reference financial services and the companies I worked for in a generic sense to gloss over the fact that I wasn't a thirty-year industry veteran. It was never an issue with my clients or teaching in *Working Women's Wealth*, but I felt insecure amongst other financial planners.

This dis-association started to come through more and more, and the "physio thing" seemed to pop up in conversations, meetings with others who had been or were physios, until it came to the wall I needed to push through.

I'd been asked to speak at the inaugural South African conference of Humans Under Management, which was established in the UK. Modelled on TED talks, we were asked to work with a speaker's coach. We agreed my topic should be on my course, "The 16 Week Side Hustle," as it was unique for a financial adviser to focus on supporting people to make money, rather than working with them to invest the money they already had. For me it was also safe. None of the other financial advisors taught people how to make more money or even raised it with their clients, whereas I believe it's a pivotal building block of a retirement plan for people who don't have enough saved—which is 94 percent of people, according to National Treasury.

Only thing was, the organiser had asked me to speak because he thought my mission to teach one million women about money was *the* unique story. I didn't know this but found out four weeks before the conference. Whilst four weeks may have been enough time to prepare a new speech, I was three days away from a surgery that would take me out of action until the day of the conference. So I told him, "Unfortunately I've been steered in the wrong direction, have already got a whole presentation done and approved, and am heading in for surgery . . . so sorry, but I can't change it."

But even I knew that my inner grumpiness about the idea of a change was a little extreme. And that's always a sign from my gut to me that there's something brewing.

Following my surgery, I had an unusual reaction to the anaesthetic and was unable to get to sleep. In the hospital, it was fine, since they give you sleeping pills, but I'm terrified of addiction, so I didn't take them when I left. And I didn't sleep.

To be honest, it was the most wonderful time with God, like He was on speaker phone. I should have journaled it all. On the third night, I never got to sleep. Not one minute. Through that night, I wrestled deeply with the issue of why I didn't want to talk about the Real Reasons for wanting to teach a million women about money.

In my work as a physical therapist, I journeyed through immense emotional trauma from working in the State Hospitals. I was at medical school at the time before Nelson Mandela became president—when there was extreme violence to secure our Free South Africa. The things I saw humanity capable of doing to each other no nineteen-year-old should ever see. As a result, I never got into a "helping" position again. One of the benefits of going into banking was that I distanced myself from the human condition. But my greatest work achievement ever that gave me the deepest sense of meaning was when I taught Mary, a patient of mine, to walk (more on that later).

I realised in the dark hours of the night that my biggest driver behind wanting to teach a million women was a desire to deeply change the lives of other humans, like I had changed the life of Mary and so many others as a physical therapist. That I had seen through my work as a financial adviser that the knowledge I and my colleagues had could set people free from worry and enable them to live their Best Life. And I could change lives without having to go back to that dark place of pain.

By the time my little twinnies woke up, I had re-written that speech in my head, messaged the organiser, and told him he was a genius—the more powerful speech was the story about teaching a million women.

When I gave the speech, it seemed to have miraculously built on the previous speeches before it, and it captured the introspective but resolute mood in the room of financial advisers—the empowering feeling that they could significantly change people's lives. I felt like I had pushed through this blockage and, for the first time, integrated these conflicting parts of me. But more importantly, I felt that because I had listened to the phone call from God by going with the harder, more vulnerable speech, I had strengthened my connection with Him.

Just two weeks later I was interviewed on Tammy Gooler Loeb's podcast about transitions,[2] where the story of my transition from physio came up again. Even though it had never been mentioned in an interview before, I was ready for it, motivated by the synchronicity, and shared openly the story I had shied away from for so many years. It was slightly jumbled and not at all polished, as I haven't spoken of physio for so long, but I was proud I crossed that barrier it seemed God had been prompting me to do.

Trusting the Timing

Listening to your gut is sometimes a long process. It was seven years from the start of my challenges in my career to the start of my financial planning journey—as gently I let go of the story The World Out There told me that to be successful you had to be CEO of a listed company. But when I look back at that journey, I know that when I did step, the time was right—emotionally, financially, and from a family perspective, as the twins were at school by then. Whilst I would have loved to have left corporate seven years before when the CEO changed, my dreams would have flopped; there was too much that needed to come together and I as a person wasn't ready yet. As much as I hate it (patience is not my gift), it sometimes takes time to get out of some very Deep Grooves and find your own path.

Sometimes that feeling in your gut is so strong, you know what you should do—but your fears keep you on the wrong path. My dad was recently needing to make a big decision and "everything inside him" was pointing *not* take the opportunity offered. But he was struggling with committing to his gut, since his sense of duty, his logic, and his rational brain felt he should say yes. He felt if he declined the opportunity, he'd be letting someone down whom he respected and admired.

Watching from the outside, it felt so clear that he should go with the loudspeaker God was using. But I could sense the struggle in him and knew that taking the step to honour his gut would be the hardest challenge of all. That first step always is. After much deliberating, he did it and wrote to decline the opportunity. What was so amazing was how supportive the person was, even voicing how he admired and respected my dad's decision to prioritise family in retirement.

Like taking the steps to honour our unique purpose, those first steps to honour our inner Wisdom instead of the logical reasons are always the hardest steps you will ever make. But I'm learning that this is such an important element of living our Best Life, which is why it's included as one of the most important parts, the protective bark, of the Support Six that make up the trunk in our Best Life Tree. And why I make you stop and think about it before you plot your next actions by including it in the action section of your Reverse Thinking Stack: Wisdom then Action.

Each day I'm practicing in small and big ways to listen more to my intuition than to the logic of The World Out There. This move to mindfulness, to being aware of the way my body reacts to circumstances, to discerning between the Good Reasons and the Real Reasons, and to using these phone calls from God are helping me read the *now* signposts in little and big ways.

JOURNALING

Throughout today, note down any time you feel a prompting to do something (or not do something), and your response. Then reflect on whether you think you should have listened to your gut or not. Each day, journal your gut prompts and phone calls from God, then look back on the week. Things you may have thought were "wrong" may in fact have been right. It's through trial and error that we figure out whether it's God's phone call or just our wishful thinking!

10

Understanding the Signposts
That Have Been

I believe deeply that you sit where you sit today for *everything* that has gone before: good and bad, things we celebrate and things we choose to hide.

Would my journey in the corporate world have been easier if I had done a business degree first and not physical therapy? Maybe. But then again, maybe not. It doesn't matter, because there truly is no way to go back and change it.

But reflection plays such a significant part in our journey. As I mentioned in chapter two, to deeply learn, the Active Learning Cycle requires us to reflect. But many of us keep our lives busy, stuck between planning and doing. Some of us stay in reflection and conclude mode but never get things done. All four are equally important.

Active Learning Cycle

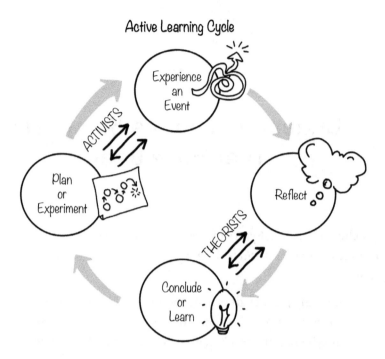

When I look back and reflect on my own journey, it really has been a lifetime of learning. I have never lived my Best Life every single day. But what's interesting about the reflection process is that it helps us to put everything in context, to see the signposts in our life that either the hurt or being in the moment somehow doesn't enable us to see.

I had an epiphany recently redoing an exercise I had previously done in 2007. The exercise is to take a clean sheet of paper and draw your journey, with its highs and lows. I chose to start close to the high point of my career, before I hit work rock bottom. For some, their journey is a straight line with little ups and downs, but mine looks like the Tour de France Map, with hills and mountains—big ups and big downs.

The Journey

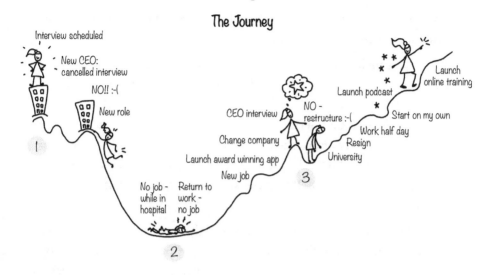

When I look back on my career, there was a definite moment when I was at the top of my corporate game (point 1). I was due for an internal interview for my absolute prize position, my biggest job ever. It was set for a Friday in February, and I was really prepared for it and excited. This was my moment to shine. I was going to step into the big league.

Then on Wednesday, two days before my big interview, the CEO of our division resigned—and with it went my job interview. He was replaced by a woman who, politely put, was not very fond of me. In a two-year period (point 2) I went from being in the top-twenty program to rock bottom, sitting at a hot desk with no job, no secretary, no office. Just a desk in the middle of the technical support team. The contrast was extreme. That journey to rock bottom really challenged everything in me. But what was harder was fighting my way out.

So why did it impact me so badly? Over time, the answer came.

My whole life I'd grown up being the good little girl, the overachiever, the hard worker. That meant that everybody out there told me how wonderful I was. And that was the problem. None of my confidence came from inside of me, from who *I* was. My confidence came from everybody else. So when the person who most mattered in the praise pile, the CEO who gave or took away jobs, chose not to have me, that was when my world crumbled.

It crumbled because I didn't have an internal strong sense of self, and I didn't have the mindset tools to deal with this rejection because, to be honest, I'd never really needed to deal with not being the best. Whilst that period of time was very far from my view of my Best Life, I always look back at it as a significant building block of what is my Best Life—since the human I am now benefited from so many different lessons. It was the sign post I needed that pointed to the future I didn't want.

The biggest lesson I learnt was the realisation that I was the same human being. I was the same human being when I was in the top twenty and I was the same human being when I was in the hot desk. My skills, my knowledge, my experience, my strengths, and my weaknesses were exactly the same. The only difference was the CEO making the decision. I learnt that my sense of who I was, my self-esteem, could not come from outside (like short-term hits of happiness); it had to come from me. But I had no idea how to build that whilst I was still in corporate.

When I left corporate, I truly had to dig deep and learn to get my sense of self, my encouragement, and my worth from me. My first challenging moment came when I launched my podcast. I don't think I'll ever forget my first interview. I felt the most unbelievable sense of imposter syndrome.

"Who am I to do a podcast?" I mean, I had never been on TV. I'd never done any broadcasting. I had no idea how to interview people.

"Who am I to launch this on iTunes?" I mean, iTunes is everywhere. Rock stars are on iTunes.

Those fears kept creeping in. "What happens if no one listens? What happens if they all think I'm an idiot? What if . . . " And the fears just engulfed me. I had no one to reassure me—most people I knew thought I was nuts. I had to back myself. I had to find the strength from within me.

After completing that journaling journey exercise, I took time to reflect, to look at the signposts, the themes in the journey, the highs and lows.

What's amazing to me is that the point I thought was the pinnacle of my career is nowhere near the high of the journey I'm currently experiencing. In The World Out There's eyes, I'm probably nowhere near as outwardly successful as I was in corporate, but to me I feel like I'm achieving far greater things. I did not consciously think as I did this. I didn't decide that something should be higher or lower in positiveness than the other. *I just drew my journey freehand and then sat back and reflected.*

Here I am a few years later, running my own business—in fact, three different businesses. I'm so far from that corporate groove I felt I would never get out of that it seems completely foreign to me to ever go back to it again. I'm doing work I love and enjoy. I choose which clients I work with. I choose which projects I do, and I love the sense of freedom and flexibility, the ability to go and watch my girls play sport or perform in a conference. All these things are priceless.

Ironically, despite how much better my work life is, I don't yet feel the same level of confidence—maybe because each new challenge brings with it a new sense of imposter syndrome. But the confidence I do have feels way more solid, more impervious to others' opinions. Don't get me wrong—I'll never fully get over the people-pleaser side of me, but my career is not reliant on one human and their thoughts of me.

JOURNALING

I encourage you to find a piece of blank paper and draw your own journey map. Spend a little time annotating it, and then sit back and reflect on it.

- What encourages you about your journey?

- Are there small little bumps or large ups and downs? There is no right or wrong—just how you experience your journey.
- Over time, are the lows lower for similar parts of your journey or are the highs higher?
- Is it getting better, or do you feel that it's getting worse and it's time to just shift where you are?
- Where are you now in relation to where you decided to start the journey?
- Then stop and ask yourself, "What do these signposts tell me about what I love doing and what I'd like to do less of?"

There's no specific place you need to start in your life. For me, I decided to start my journey map at the high of corporate. Maybe you decided to start your journey from when you were a child.

Each time I do this exercise with clients in my "Brave to Be Free" courses, it so often springs an "Ah-Ha" moment. Karen, one attendee of the course, said, "When I did my life journey, I saw how a pivotal event in my life a few years ago gave me the courage to embark on my current journey. That event was in 2013, and it took six years to build the courage and support system to leave academic medicine, cut back on my clinical practice, and start the journey of a digital nomad!"

What's Brought You Joy?

When it comes to working out what your superpower is, what the things you enjoy are, and which periods of life you've really benefited from, it's so important to look back at this journey and get a deep understanding of why you sit here in this seat today. The biggest question is, what are you learning? Because that's what this journey of life is about—to learn, to grow, to be the best version of you possible.

While preparing to write this book, I recently did a similar exercise with my book coach. In this one, I mapped out the big phases of my life on a horizontal timeline. I drew the enjoyable phases of life above the timeline and those that weren't so great, below. I managed to fit my whole life onto two A4 sheets!

Life Line

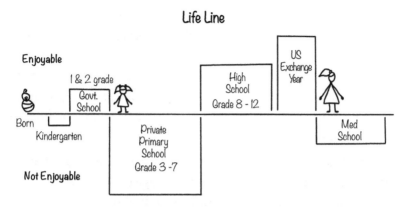

My big Ah-Ha insight was around the experiences I perceived as positive. I have attended four schools and three universities. My best experiences were those where the classes were diverse—in culture or background or financial means.

My first and second grades were spent at the local government school, and I did a year after I finished school as an exchange student at a local school in Sheboygan, Wisconsin. I loved those experiences, loved the diversity, and felt so much less pressure to be something I wasn't. In contrast, my time at private junior school was difficult—everyone there was from the city, from wealthy backgrounds. I loved my high school—despite being a private school, it was in a tiny town surrounded by farmlands. This meant the girls from the city, like me, were in the minority, and the girls from the farms or smaller district towns were the majority. But it still didn't feel as free as the diverse open schools I went to.

Same thing for medical school—whilst there was great diversity in means and background, everyone there was exceptionally clever. It was like we'd all come out of the same cookie cutter. And for the first time, I felt like "the weakest link." Why? Because what had made me stand out in the past, my academic ability, was now just an entry criterion to the game, and I hadn't fully developed self-confidence in other areas to feel good about myself in the absence of being one of the best academically. When compared to my classmates at medical school, I felt dumb.

The insight was powerful in helping me understanding when I felt I fitted in and when I felt I belonged. This makes me more mindful now of seeking out opportunities where I belong—diverse environments of different humans with different interests, different views, and different strengths. It also makes me conscious of when I'm trying to fit in—when I believe everyone else is better than me or in "competition" for similar things.

There's a wonderful TED talk by Margaret Heffernan that references the work of an evolutionary biologist called William Muir from Purdue University. He wanted to study productivity, so he did an experiment to see what would make chickens more productive in laying eggs.

He created one group of the most productive egg-laying chickens, which he called Super Chickens, and left them alone for six generations. Each new generation, he selected only the most productive for breeding to engineer a Super Flock. At the end, he compared them to another group of mixed-ability, average chickens, who were left to do their thing.

The results were astonishing.

The Average Flock had flourished—they were plump and fully feathered, and egg production had increased significantly. On the other hand, the Super Chickens had pecked each other to death and just three survived. They had only achieved their success by suppressing the productivity of the rest.

Margaret's comments on that story re-enforced my big Ah-Ha moment:

> "Now, as I've gone around the world talking about this and telling this story in all sorts of organizations and companies, people have seen the relevance almost instantly, and they come up and they say things to me like, 'That Super Flock, that's my company. . . .' For the past fifty years, we've run most organizations and some societies along the Super Chicken model. We've thought that success is achieved by picking the superstars . . . and giving them all the resources and all the

power. And the result has been just the same as in William Muir's experiment: aggression, dysfunction, and waste."[1]

She goes on to describe an MIT experiment that concluded three key characteristics present for successful teams:

1. They show high degrees of social sensitivity to each other (empathy).
2. They gave roughly equal time to each other, and no one voice dominated, nor were there any "passengers," as she called them.
3. They had more women on the team. The researchers couldn't say whether this is because women naturally have more empathy or whether the sheer element of diversity added to the cohesiveness of the team.

These principles mirrored my enjoyment of my schools and my workplaces. The teams I loved had a high degree of respect and trust and a high degree of diversity—of age, race, background, gender. The leaders focused on hearing everyone's voice, the mutual standards of respect and delivery were high, and passengers who didn't contribute were gently nudged out.

JOURNALING

Take a step back and timeline each of the phases of your whole life, placing positive experiences on the top of the line, and negative or less positive ones under the line. For me, I simply asked myself, "Was this an above- or below-the-line experience?" No overthinking.

Then step back.

- What do the above-the-line experiences have in common? What do the below-the-line experiences have in common?
- Do you need to dig deeper and do either Five Whiskeys and a Heineken or a Reverse Thinking Stack?

What Work Makes You Happy?

A final exercise that was extremely powerful for me was looking at what work made me happy. It came from Pat Flynn's book *Will It Fly?*[2] I've modified the questions over time to help my course participants gain deeper insight. I thought about each job I'd had and asked myself the following questions:

1. What did you enjoy about it?
2. What didn't you enjoy?
3. What was your favourite memory?
4. What were the Good Reasons you gave for leaving, and what were the Real Reasons?

Through this exercise, I saw patterns and trends reflecting the types of situations that make me happy, give me energy, give me pride. But it surprised me to see what achievement I'm most proud of, since it is contrary to what The World Out There said it should be.

I've had some truly amazing opportunities in my career and consider myself one of the luckiest humans in the world. In 2000, in my first company after physio, I was the product manager that worked with a team of phenomenal humans to launch the world's third mobile bank ever, the first with full-bank-level security, which we developed together with Nokia. I was just twenty-four.

Later that year I found myself as Head of Strategy for a six-billion-pound business unit in the UK. At twenty-eight, I was the integration lead on the deal team that bought an eighty-million-Pound company, and I managed the integration of that business into our own. I ran a R3bn business unit at thirty-five and at thirty-nine designed an app that went on to win a global award for big data banking app of the year.

But none of that compares with an achievement that I think will forever remain my proudest. Why? Because whilst I worked hard for each one of them, with many long nights and weekends with huge emotional tolls, not one of them truly changed the life of another human.

My biggest career success, the achievement I am most proud about, was teaching Mary to walk when I was a student physical therapist.

Mary had an autoimmune disease called Systemic Lupus Erythematosis, or SLE. Essentially, the disease was shutting down her nervous system, and she was effectively paralysed. When I met her, she lay in the bed with a nappy on, since she had lost the use of the nerves that controlled her bladder. Of all the things the disease had taken away, the nappy was her worst because of the humiliation she felt as an adult having to lie in a soiled nappy until a nurse could clean it.

Mary was exceptionally lucky that her type of SLE was responding well to a new drug, and her body was fighting back to regain nerve usage. The trouble was, her muscles had completely atrophied from lack of use. So no matter how much the drugs worked, without the physio, she would still lie limp. As a student, I only had four weeks to work with her before my rotation ended.

Mary was one of those people who creeps into your heart. I became so determined to help her that I came in at 6:30 a.m. every morning to give her an hour of one-on-one time before ward rounds at 7:30 a.m. For a third-year student who had to leave home at 6:00 a.m. to get to Soweto—the township outside of Johannesburg—you must know how special she was.

Within the first week, we restored her ability to control her bladder and bowel. As she realised she could control her bladder and bowel, tears rolled down her soft cheeks with pride and gratitude. It made me even more determined to help her become independent.

Each week we got a little more of her back.

On my final day, the nurse wouldn't allow me into the ward until all was ready. Then I was led in, blindfolded. As I opened my eyes, there at the opposite side of the ward, with a nurse carefully behind her, was Mary. She walked the full stretch of the ward, unaided, toward me. By the time she got to me, there was not a dry eye in the ward as Mary and I sobbed, hugging each other, humbled by the miracle that had taken place.

As I did those three journaling exercises, I realised what I was missing in my life. My experiences with physio and with Mary have been powerful signposts that have shed light on what truly makes me happy.

Unlike the crap The World Out There told me, the things that make me happy are not money-related, not climbing the corporate ladder, not being with everyone who looks and is the same as me. The things that make me happy, truly happy, are usually never shouted about on Instagram by The World Out There. They were:

- Using my talents to help others and change their lives.
- Spending time with diverse groups of people who aren't competing for career or social supremacy, who are each on their own journey, who are encouraging me on mine.
- Be open to the idea that the "peak" of your career or happiness may just be a point on the road. That growing yourself, finding your voice, and being brave may lead to a far greater joy in life than any achievements The World Out There told you would bring you happiness.

Looking backward has helped me see the signposts that point to the experiences, people, and teams I need to create going forward in order to live MY Best Life.

JOURNALING

Think back on your jobs, and answer the four questions:

1. What did you enjoy about it?
2. What didn't you enjoy?
3. What is your favourite memory?
4. What were the Good Reasons you gave for leaving, and what were the Real Reasons?
    - For this you may need to dig deeper and do either Five Whiskeys and a Heineken or a Reverse Thinking Stack

Then step back and reflect, writing the answer to this question: What have been your biggest Ah-Has of these three exercises?

11

Understanding the
Signposts That Are Now

Feel the Fear and Do It Anyway is the title of a book I love by Susan Jeffers. What I love about the title is that it starts by acknowledging that we all feel fear. There's no pop psychology that if we live in the light, we will not fear. If we stretch ourselves, we will fear. We do fear. And if we're not fearing, it's because that reptilian brain of ours has kept us so safely snug in our Deep Groove that we are not challenging ourselves. I love this quote from the book:

> "Whenever we take a chance and enter unfamiliar territory or put ourselves into the world in a new way, we experience fear. Very often this fear keeps us from moving ahead with our lives. The trick is to FEEL THE FEAR AND DO IT ANYWAY. . . . So many of us short-circuit our living by choosing the path that is the most comfortable."[1]

When I decided to start my podcast, I did what I always do: I invested money that hurt, bought an online course by a podcaster I admired, and went through all the lessons. I ordered the equipment and for a very long time I did nothing. I was ready to go, but I did nothing.

Why? I was absolutely racked with fear because I was stepping into new territory, where the tribe of successful, public personalities lived. The tribe where your successes were shouted about and your failures were on record for the world to see. This was a very unfamiliar groove that I had no idea about—no real understanding of the lay of the land, no knowledge of whether the groove had enemies I wouldn't be able to fight. Nothing. At least when I left corporate, I was under the radar, and if I saw my old colleagues and they asked how my business was going, I'd be able to tell them how wonderful it was, and they'd be none the wiser. But when I launched this podcast and put my show in the public for everybody to hear, they and everyone else who stood in the stands of life could look at me in the arena and boo, laugh, and throw rocks at my efforts.

As I've said, we need to feel the fear because it's part of our brain's ancient protective mechanisms. It's one of those brain responses that we need to feel it, acknowledge it, but then use our upper brain to choose *not* to give in to it and do what it is that we're fearing anyway. But it does give us a wonderful signpost we can use positively if we're mindful enough to notice the fear and use it to our advantage—and not run back to the safety of our groove.

Susan categorises two levels of fear: fear of things that happen and ego-related fears.

Within the level one fears (things that happen), there are two different types of fears:

The first one is *situational fears*—things that **will happen,** regardless of whether you want it or not, something that we have no control over. Many people fear aging. Many people fear being retired from their company (one I see all the time). Many people fear being alone. They fear their children leaving home and what they will do when that happens. A loved one dying, a natural disaster. Any of these fears are going to happen—regardless of what you do. And so worrying about them won't change whether it happens or not.

The second is *fears within our sphere of control*, but they won't come into being if we **don't act**. We can avoid them by not acting. These are things like going back to study, the fear of making a decision, changing careers, making friends, ending or starting a relationship, public speaking, asserting oneself, losing weight, driving, broadcasting. If we don't resign from our job or don't go out and find another job, we won't change careers. These are the fears that keep us in our comfort zone.

Level two fears are *all about ego.*

They are fears that are hidden from the world and happen inside us. The challenge is that whilst no one can see them, sometimes we don't either. These fears reflect how we think we'll be able to handle the world we live in. By nature, these fears permeate everything we do. These are things like the fear of rejection, of success, of failing, of being vulnerable, of being conned, of helplessness, of loss of image.

For these, our perception of our ability to handle this world that we live in permeates everything that we do. Why? Because they reflect how we think we'll be able to cope with these particular situations. I love this question that Susan asks:

> "If you knew that you could handle anything that came your way, what would you possibly have to fear?"[2]

It really is such an interesting question to spend some time pondering and journaling.

My greatest fear in my new career is that I'm going to say something dumb in a live environment, something I don't mean that comes out wrong. And once said, it will be recorded forever, slated on social media, and overshadow the millions of right things I may say. My fear is that the pain and shame will be so great, I will never recover. It will rip my heart in two, and Cruella de Vil will torture me for months and years after. Her cruel voice will tell me:

- You are so stupid.
- See, I told you not to step into the arena.
- You say you didn't mean it, but it must be somewhere in your heart. That proves you are a mean and horrible human.
- Just crawl back under the desk where you belong. Give it up.

The other cornerstone question I regularly ask when faced with fears is, "What is the worst that could happen?" This question gets followed at least four times with "And then what . . . ?" or the Five Whiskeys and a Heineken test.

So let's use the example above:

> The worst that will happen in my 'public' career is that I will say something that truly comes out the wrong way and I will be humiliated again and again on media or social media.

And then what happens?

Well, many people who do not know me will jump in and think I am an awful human. And people who know me will all be talking about me behind my back at dinner parties and in school car parks.

And then what happens?

I will lose my friends and hang my head in shame.

And then what happens?

It will hurt so much. I will jump on the couch next to John, crawl under his arm, and cry my heart out.

And then what happens?

He will tell me he loves me, whatever I've said. That he knows my heart and knows me deeply and knows that I truly didn't mean what I said. My little girls will give me a hug and tell me they love me. So will my broader family. Actually, so will most of my closest friends—even if I lose one through this process, I'll probably keep at least one or two.

And then what happens?

I'll pick myself up and keep moving on. Those true members of my tribe will believe my explanation of the event and will respect me for owning it. And those who weren't true members will leave. And the tribe left will be stronger, filled with the 'faithfuls' who are with me on the journey, no matter what.

By the time I get here, I've faced my worst fear in the eye. I've felt its hurt and pain. So I keep on podcasting, speaking, being interviewed live. Why? Because in the end, we are built to survive. It's been wired in us over the centuries. And we will pick ourselves up and keep slaying dragons. That is what we do. But by deeply thinking about the ramifications of the fear and the shame that could happen, I can see that it will be a horrible experience but, in the end, will work out OK.

The biggest question we need to keep asking ourselves is, "Is the fear proportional to the real threat?"

When I think about my decision to leave the corporate world and go on my own, it was truly one of the toughest decisions I have ever made. I was deeply situated in the corporate groove—it's all I'd ever known—and it was my identity, my ambition, and my goal to prove to The World Out There that I was the best of the best by becoming CEO of a major corporation. So to step off that ladder felt like giving up, admitting defeat, losing. A complete loss of identity. Cutting my little boat off from the big ship—its status, its protection, and its provision.

But when I did this exercise, the worst that could possibly happen was my new business failing, us losing some money, and me swallowing my pride and getting a job back in corporate.

Is that worst case really proportional to the huge fears that so nearly won the battle and kept me in corporate for such a long time—depriving me of finding my joy and purpose?

No. And I thank God daily that I never allowed those fears to chain me to my comfort zone, to that groove. Our assumptions of what may happen, of the pain we will feel, of how debilitatingly crushing it will be are elephants in our head but mice when we shine a light on them, when we voice them, put them on the table, wrestle with them.

I've thought deeply about Marianne Williamson's quote, and I've come to agree with her that I do deeply fear being successful.

It's not that I fear success in and of itself. But I fear that when I am successful, it may lead to too many people wanting something from me, to expectations I'm not able to fulfill. You see, I already get people asking me to mentor them or 'just' meet with them for a coffee or 'just' have a quick chat with their friend. And whilst I'd love to mentor the world and I'd love to chat to everybody, I physically also need time in my day to see my clients, do my work, and create my content to teach. I need time to spend with my daughters, John, and my family and friends. And most of all, I need time alone to recharge my batteries.

And so I end up disappointing people because there's not enough time for all of that and them.

These kinds of boundaries are hard for me, and I fear a loss of reputation or 'image,' as Susan calls it. The story I tell myself is that people will say, "You know what? Now that she's all successful, she can't even take the time of day to meet with someone normal."

The reality is that we need boundaries. But people don't like boundaries, being told no. "Actually, no, I don't have the time to see your friend. It's not because I think anything less of them, it's because I have to respect the space and boundaries that I need in order to continue to do the work I do." And whilst I think saying that should be OK, the people-pleaser in me has a complete heart attack and hides under the table. Why? Because it's amazing how nasty humans can be when they don't get their way.

Using Fear as a Signpost

Fears are our 'now' signposts. They help us know right now what is stopping us from living our Best Life. If I don't explore this fear of the implications of success, my subconscious and all its eleven million bits per second will broadcast those fears and ensure I don't become successful. The key to using fear as a lesson is not to use it as yet another whip to beat ourselves up.

Our goal needs to be to recognise it, to sit down with it in a non-judgemental way, and to learn as much as it will tell us about our Real Reasons for fearing something, not our Good Reasons. But our Real Reasons will never surface in the presence of judgement. They require gentleness to speak their truth, something my Cruella de Vil is not very good at doing.

But how do we know when our fears show their face?

For this I turn again to the true master, Brené Brown. One of my favourites of her books is *The Gifts of Imperfection*—maybe that's because I'm not yet advanced enough in my own walk to Dare Greatly, Rise Strong, or go Into the Wilderness.

She encapsulates so much in this one paragraph:

> "*If shame is the universal fear of being unworthy of love and belonging, and if all people have an irreducible and innate need to experience love and belonging, it's easy to see why shame is often referred to as 'the master emotion.'* **We don't have to experience**

shame to be paralyzed by it—the fear of being perceived as
unworthy is enough to force us to silence our stories."[3]

The first step is to be aware of those fears, that feeling of shame, and how they present for you. As I've mentioned earlier, for me there is a crushing sensation at the top of my stomach and the bottom of my chest, like an elephant is sitting on my cleavage. Sometimes it's just a sensation, sometimes it's uncomfortable, and sometimes it crushes the breath out of me.

But in *The Gifts of Imperfection*, Brené sites the work of Dr. Hartling of the Stone Center at Wellesley. She says that we,

- "Move away by withdrawing, hiding, silencing ourselves, and keeping secrets . . .
- Move toward by seeking to appease and please . . .
- Move against by trying to gain power over others, by being aggressive, and by using shame to fight shame."[4]

Brené refers to these as our Shame Shields, what we put on to protect ourselves from the fear, hurt, and pain. The problem with these shields is how often, when I look back at my day, I have used all three of them. How I've withdrawn from situations because I've pre-assumed that people won't like me. How I've spent so much of my day trying to please people and appease situations. And how, especially when I'm tired, I can use aggression and power to counter my own fears.

Remember the story of when I noticed I was trying to fit in to the financial adviser's network? I was using 'trying to please.' One of the ways I try and fit in and please is by oversharing, so my action I committed to after trying to please was that at the lunch I would only speak if I truly had something meaningful to contribute—and not overshare. Reflecting back on that lunch, I think I'd score myself eight out of ten for *not* using an oversharing shield.

What was interesting was that although I was being more my true self, I actually had to try hard to think about not oversharing, to check my thoughts. Because I've spent my whole entire life trying to fit in, that it is my unconscious habit. So I have to go through that horrible 'learning to ride the bike phase' of conscious incompetence at practicing being me!

JOURNALING

The first step to seeing your Today Signposts are

1. Learn how and when you feel fear or shame.
2. Observe how and when you shield yourself.
3. Be gentle and mindful enough (*without* criticism, judgement, and Cruella) to enter into a dialogue with it. Ask it:
    a. What is the worst that can happen?
    b. And if you knew that you could in fact handle anything that came your way, would you still allow fear to cast such a long shadow in your life?

Start by looking back at the last day or week and noticing if you've withdrawn or silenced yourself, if or when you've people-pleased, or when you were aggressive. Write down that incident in detail using the following feedback formula, as if you were giving feedback to yourself in the kindest, gentlest way:

- What did you see? Write it as if it was a video and you were narrating the whole scene to someone on the phone.
- How did that make you feel? You can use Brené's formula of "The story I'm telling (I told myself) is / was . . ."

Then pause and deeply go through questioning your Thinking Stack using either Five Whiskeys and a Heineken or the Reverse Thinking Stack.

12

Looking from the Outside In

recently heard the most wonderful quote: "You can't read the label from inside the jar!" And it's so true.

Sometimes, especially if we are in a rough place or trying to push through the detail, we are unable to see the signposts as clearly as everyone else can. What is sometimes right in front of our nose is invisible to us.

Understanding our superpowers, seeing our patterns of behaviour, and understanding our blind spots is often best supported by the feedback of a diverse circle of friends, family, bosses, subordinates, and colleagues. We must remember, however, that their view of us is often shaped by their own issues, their own Thinking Stacks.

Early on in my return to South Africa, I got a job at a local bank. I was finishing off a project for Citibank Europe, remote working from their South Africa office. My young, strong, determined soon-to-be employee from the local bank decided that before this new boss of hers joined, she would come over to Citibank to see for herself what I was about. It struck me as odd, but I was totally happy to oblige. We met in the canteen, shared a cappuccino, and she left.

Her early career had been at Capital One in South Africa, and so the culture of feedback was completely normal to her. I, however, had not been exposed to a genuine feedback culture. So you can imagine my horror when a few weeks into my employment she volunteered to me that whilst she loved working for me now, her first impression of me was that she thought I was one of 'those bra-burning bitches' and that 'the softest thing about me was my teeth'!

I have often been given the feedback that I come across as laser-focussed on the results needed, with an exceptionally high standard of delivery, and not much of the warm and fuzzies. I've always struggled with the view that the softest thing about me was my teeth—because I live with me, and I see myself as the softest marshmallow on the planet, a people-pleasing puppy desperate for everyone to like me and who gets deeply hurt at the slightest challenge. I wish I were more hard-arsed, don't-give-a-shit in a genuine way—I think life would be way easier. To be honest, I never quite knew what they meant by those comments, since I lived with my insecure view of me.

That feedback has always been totally at odds with other feedback from people who've worked for me and who have said how deeply I care, how loyal I am to them, and how committed I am to their growth and development. Yes, I have high expectations, but they see them in the context of a person genuinely backing their careers.

Having been in the corporate world for so long now, I have been subjected to most of the personality / thinking / behavioural profiles there are, and various types of 360-degree review processes. One of my last 360 reviews was facilitated by a person who was clearly brilliant (she was an ex-McKinsey Consultant) but was also completely batty, and she drove me nuts. But she used a tool I'd never been exposed to, which is always intellectually interesting for me.

Following a very large sample of people—from my boss, subordinates, colleagues, and broader project teams—I met with her, my walls definitely up. I couldn't have been more wrong, as the tool and her feedback were exceptionally insightful.

My key Ah-Ha moment that put those years of feedback into context came from the huge disparity in comments between those on the periphery (the project teams) and those close to me (my boss and subordinates). Those close to me scored me a level 4.5 out of 5 leader. To them, I was collaborative, unselfish, inspirational. But as the circle got farther apart—to colleagues, their teams, and the project teams—my scores dropped.

The data gave me a way to understand the huge difference in feedback I'd received for so long. That young subordinate's first impression of me was that the softest thing about me was my teeth. Yet that same woman now, having worked both for me and as a colleague and now friend, would go to war with me, and I with her. The insight has made me understand more about how others' more infrequent in their interactions with me see me—and how important it is for me to take the time to get to know people, to show them who I am.

Since that initial bra-burning moment, I have learned to cherish feedback—from trusted sources—as a way to hone my skills, sharpen my saw. Treat the people whose feedback you cherish as gold. Not the ones who just tell you you're wonderful, but those who will give you the honest truth with the genuine intention of making you better but who also would back you in a war if need be. They'll tell you the Real Reasons, not the Good Reasons for something, or they'll help you think through something until you get to the Real Reasons.

Be Clear If They Are in the Arena

But I've also learned that not all feedback is good feedback, and not all feedback should be cherished. In fact, most of us need to be *way* more discerning about whose feedback we listen to, who we allow to look into our jar and tell us what our labels say to them.

As Theodore Roosevelt says in his amazing speech, given in France in 1910,

> *"It is not the critic who counts; not the man who points out how the strong man stumbles, or where the doer of deeds could have done them better. The credit belongs to the man who is actually in the arena, whose face is marred by dust and sweat and blood; who strives valiantly; who errs, and comes short again and again, because there is no effort without error and shortcoming; but who does actually strive to do the deeds; who knows the great enthusiasms, the great devotions; who spends himself in a worthy cause; who at the best knows in the end the*

triumph of high achievement, and who at the worst, if he fails, at least fails while daring greatly, so that his place shall never be with those cold and timid souls who know neither victory nor defeat."[1]

So I always ask myself,

1. Is this feedback coming from someone in the arena or someone in the grandstands?
2. Do I believe they truly have my best interests at heart?

If they don't, you need to be very circumspect when taking their feedback to heart. Their feedback can often hurt you, but it helps to remember that they're just flawed human beings, acting out their own Real Reasons, justifying why they stay small and miserable.

Too often, I see people who have taken to heart the criticism of The World Out There, or people in the grandstands, or gladiators intent on destroying them to better their own position. Over time those words act as the heaviest of burdens that keep us stuck in those Deep Grooves of living a life so far from the Best Life we imagined.

Another song that deeply resonates with me that I put on at full blast and scream the words from the bottom of my tummy as I fly down the highway is "This is Me," sung by Kesha, from the movie *The Greatest Showman.*

When I think of these amazing women who've lost sight of their amazing gifts and talents, their joy, the first verse comes to mind:

> *I am not a stranger to the dark*
> *Hide away, they say*
> *'Cause we don't want your broken parts*
> *I've learned to be ashamed of all my scars*
> *Run away, they say*
> *No one will love you as you are.*[2]

How true are those words—that for some reason, we have all been taught by The World Out There to be ashamed of our scars. Why? So many of our scars come from bad decisions we made before we were twenty-five, before the frontal lobe of our brain was fully formed, before we were able to use our full powers of reasoning to fight with that teenage developing brain that caused so much chaos. Other scars were inflicted by circumstances outside our control or by other humans who were broken by their own pain.

When I see the strength and talent I know lives in every human, I want to call into the hearts of each one, and myself, and tell them, "God made you an amazing human! God made you talented! Don't listen to all the broken souls chained down by their own pain! Listen to that Still Small Voice inside you that's whispering, 'RISE UP . . . get up . . . be brave . . . find your strength.'"

I know that so many of us feel far from being able to rise up and be strong—or, as the song goes on to say, that we are able to truly march to the beat we drum. We are concerned about what everyone else expects or thinks of us. But those words need to call each of us out. As if crouched down on the floor, that brave, young, hopeful soul of our youth rises strong from our hearts, leading us to the destiny we were created for.

Braveheart Warrior Princess Rising

As you ask others for their feedback, remember this: *Each of us was born with gifts and talents and with parts of us that are less than ideal. But that doesn't make us ALL bad or ALL good.*

The Inner Critic

We cannot let The World Out There and the critic within us *ever* tell us that we are mostly made up of the less-than-ideal parts. It's utter crap. We are mostly made up of gifts, talents, and the goodness of humanity. When receiving feedback, most of us will gloss over the good things people say about us and focus all our attention and heartache on the 'areas of improvement' that they give us.

Are we flawed? Have we messed up? Absolutely. But if we were to do a count-up every day, we definitely score more than 50 percent on the test of goodness. We just tend to weight that one mess up way more than the gazillion other good things. Let go of that. Shut up the Cruella de Vil voice in your head. The longer you repeat that beating up, the more it becomes deeply rooted in your subconscious as part of your identity.

When my daughter Jess was six, she was bullied at school and we decided to take her to a self-esteem therapist. When asked to say the good things about herself, she had nothing to say, not one thing. So the therapist asked me to start the process off. I said she was kind.

"No, Mama," she said, "I'm not kind. Yesterday I was mean to Isi and Emma."

The therapist then asked her, "Is your mum kind?"

"She's very kind," Jess responded.

"But yesterday, Mama was tired and ratty from work, and she was not very kind to Dada," I replied. "Does that make me an unkind person?"

"No, Mama," she said. "You had a bad day."

Isn't it amazing how we can see the humanity in others, but we don't give ourselves the grace and gentleness or allow the humanity in ourselves? I had spent the last twenty-four hours beating myself up about what an unkind awful human I was to John, and it took the mirror of my daughter to show me how cruel and graceless the voice in our head can be.

Understanding Your Superpower

So if someone you trust gives you an area of improvement, go gently on beating yourself up.

The most helpful exercise we can do is to ask those around what our superpowers are and look back at our life to connect the dots. Understanding your superpower is crucial to understanding what work or philanthropy you should do and where you should spend your time. Why? Because when we incorporate our superpower into our work we will *always* be great at what we do. It's no point being a process engineer when your superpower is sales.

We are all terrible at seeking and receiving positive feedback. But if you truly want to see one of the strongest signposts to the things that will help you live your Best Life, go engage with people from all parts of your life and ask them about what they think your superpower is. And be sure to listen with an open heart.

Every person whom I've ever supported doing this superpower exercise in my course "Brave to Be Free" always tells me what a truly humbling and strengthening exercise it is. Many describe how they hate putting together the email that asks for the feedback or setting up the conversation, but the outcome has never been less than transformational for any of them.

Some find the feedback consistent, and others find different people highlight very different things. Your work colleagues may see some superpowers that your friends don't see, and vice versa.

Your superpower is often that thing that you can do unconsciously well that you don't think of as a superpower. For me that was explaining complicated things in a simple, human way. When I did this exercise, I wasn't surprised by the feedback—but what did surprise me was that something I did so naturally was seen by others as a superpower. When you integrate your superpower into your work, your life, and your efforts to serve others, that's when you create uniqueness and joy in your world. It's when you hum. That's why the teaching I do, the content I write, is stuff I really enjoy and do well at—because it's rooted in my superpower. The most common feedback I get from my wealth management clients is how it's the first time they've ever understood their finances and how the steps will lead them to their goals and Best Life.

We are so busy beating ourselves up—in addition to the beatings life gives us—that so much of our headspace is taken up by criticism. When others hold the mirror to you and show you the good they see, it is a gift we need to deeply engage with and be open to believing. It's *their* truth. When you can't see it, don't dismiss it. Believe them and try find events in your life that could back up their view of your superpowers and gifts.

JOURNALING

Email at least ten very different people, and tell them that you're receiving coaching and have been asked to get feedback from different people in answer to the question, "What's my superpower?"

Then journal their feedback, and what you think of it.

- Does it resonate?
- If not, why not?
    - » If you have no idea where they would get that from, step into their shoes. Can you think of an interaction you've had with that person that may cause them to give you that feedback?

» If you struggle with the self-confidence to believe the 'compliment' (it is in fact their reality, not a compliment), then you need to go back and do five Whiskeys and a Heineken or the Reverse Thinking Stack exercise.

» Then think of how you can integrate your superpower even more into your life and work to find more joy and give more joy to others.

Testing

Another opportunity we have to look at the labels outside our jars is through thinking / behavioural / personality tests. Each one of these different tests looks at a human from a different perspective—sometimes overlapping, sometimes different—each teaching us something different. Some, such as HBDI (Hermann Brain Dominance Instrument, which I am certified to administer), look at our thinking styles, based on the belief that our thinking determines our actions. Others look at our personality or our behaviour.

If we choose to engage with them, these tests can be exceptionally powerful in the facilitation of real conversations, rather than the good conversations we have with people around us. Each one of these tests group large amounts of data from many individuals' thinking or behaviour to get a 'norm' for different types of thinking or behaving. Many times they give us an insight into how we think and behave not only at our best, but also under stress, and the blind spots or gaps we may have.

The results of these tests provide us with a language, a short code for something with deeper meaning. I call these Suitcase Phrases because these tiny words enable us to find a way to unoffensively communicate in a neat suitcase tons of meaning you don't need to explicitly put into the conversation.

These generalisations of behavioural or thinking characteristics and Suitcase Phrases together enable us to say things to someone without causing defensiveness or shame. One of my good friends and previous coach, Mel, is also an HBDI practitioner and deeply committed to the benefits of feedback. In HBDI, I score low on the Relational Red quadrant—which shows itself when people think the softest thing about me is my teeth. But I score high on its opposite, the Analytical Blue.

When I was giving Mel feedback on her financial plan, she was able to say to me, "Lisa, you need a whole lot more Red when you do this." This one small Suitcase Phrase was filled with understanding and unoffensively communicated feedback that enabled me to hone my craft.

What I love about HBDI is the underlying belief that you can access *all* parts of your brain. You may have a preference, such as being a right-footed kicker, but with practice, you can become proficient at left-footed kicking. These preferences only fall short if you use them as an excuse: "Well, I'm just not Red Relational, so people need to suck it up."

I recently re-did the Enneagram test as part of a financial coaching program I was doing with other financial advisers. Because I had spent a lot of money on the program, I decided that when the feedback came, I would engage with it in an open-minded way. At one point, the results of my stress profile indicated that my main stressor was my physical environment. When I read the descriptor, it sounded like a description for someone living in a UK or US city, with neighbours close by. My instinct was to ignore it—I live in a large house with a large lawn and pool, and I very seldom ever even hear my neighbours except when their gardeners are mowing their lawn.

But because I'd made the commitment to not brush anything off, I thought deeply about this and realised that it was absolutely accurate. I am *not* good at admin. I can do it, and I can especially do it for work, but I hate the admin of getting someone to fix the dishwasher, dealing with the gate motor struck by lightning, or addressing the leaking roof. It is my biggest stress, the never-ending to-do list of the house, my physical environment.

HBDI has the ability to do a 'Pairs Profile,' which helps any two people see their thinking styles side-by-side. It always elicits a profound Ah-Ha in both people and gives them a common language going forward.

Having external mirrors to show you what they see about you—both great superpowers and possible detractors—enables you to see signposts today that can help you to look back and connect the dots. Using the signposts to plan your path going forward requires you to be open to the feedback, remembering that it *always* comes from the lens of that human giving it. And when you know your superpowers and detractors, you can aim to leverage your strengths and install safety nets to limit the impact of your detractors.

JOURNALING

If you have ever done a 360 review or a personality, behavioural, or thinking assessment, dig it out and have a look again at it.

If you don't and you'd like to do an HBDI assessment for yourself (or a pairs profile with your partner) go to www.LisaLinfield.com /HBDI.

Take the report you have and, together with your previous journaling, look at how the strengths and detractors in your report support or challenge the pathway you'd like to be on.

Answer the following questions:

- Do you resonate with the commentary of the strengths or thinking styles or behaviours?
- Looking at your superpowers, what is supported by your strengths?
- How did the phases of your life you enjoyed and the positive portions of your journey map leverage your strengths?

Then look at your detractors and go through the same exercise.

13

Permission to Dream

The first time I launched my "Brave to Be Free" course, the section on your vision for your future was 'innovatively' titled, "Creating Your Vision." I gave everyone the exercise to dream in a totally unconstrained manner and gave them permission not to worry about idealistic sentimentalities or real-life constraints like selfless parenthood, prioritising others, work, or financial limitations. The goal was to just dream, as free as possible, to not think about anyone else's needs, just you and your dreams. Like when you were a child. I told them that the minute they felt a 'but' or a 'can't,' they were to hush it, to park it to the side, knowing we'd get to those, but that this time was to allow the space to just dream.

One of my first group of course participants from Australia, Del, wrote to me and said, "I liked that idea of dreaming without constraint first up, the permission to do it. I am always caught up in why I *can't* possibly do something, so to have that taken away and to just think about *my* dream was a really good exercise." She was echoed by another participant, Tori, who said, "The dreaming took longer than I'd anticipated but has definitely reawakened parts of me that I had been 'hushing' in favour of realism and real-life obligation."

Why is it that we have lost the ability to dream?

I think both Del and Tori give us such profound insight in their responses. We've become so conditioned by The World Out There to favour logic and realism and putting others' needs first (especially as women), and we've been so beaten down by life and our perceived failures that we have stopped or postponed *our* dreams to make space for the dreams of our partners, children, and family. Maybe those failed attempts, or the words from The World Out There have even taken us to the place of believing that we can't achieve our dreams. Our focus is the now, the 'real-life obligations' that make dreaming feel like an impractical, unachievable waste of time.

The Key to Achieving Goals

But if we're always looking at the next step immediately in front of us and never look up to see if we're heading in the direction we want to go, how will we ever change the path we are on?

The brain science and years of research on goal setting is clear and unanimous: the bigger the goal, the better we will perform, and the happier we will feel. One of the pioneers of research into goal setting, Professor Edwin Locke, identified two key elements on goals:

1. It must be specific and clear
2. It must be a challenge—easy or tedious goals are demotivating. The higher or harder the goal, the more energy becomes available to be invested in achieving that goal.[1]

So if we don't set goals—or if our goals become the to-do list of the chores for the next day—we are going to end up feeling life is tedious and demotivating, and that leads to feeling low in energy, low in hope, and low in optimism.

Now, one of the most amazing things I've discovered in my research is that one of the highest determinants of success is hope. Not IQ, hope. One of the cornerstones of thinking on hope is Rick Snyder. In his seminal article on Hope Theory, he built on the basic notion of what hope is—"an overall perception that goals can be met"—by giving us the key ingredients of how to make hope be a more powerful driver in our success.

- The first principle is **agency**—or the belief that I personally own the goals, and I have the opportunity to direct the successful outcome (e.g., it's not a goal I've been given by someone else with no way on earth of ever achieving it).

- The second principle is our **ability to find successful pathways** to achieve our goals.[2]

So the more we own our goals and believe that we can find a path to achieve our goals, the more hope we will have of achieving those goals.

For me, hope was one of those cheesy words that were carved into wood, whitewash painted, and nailed to walls in homes. I truly never understood people's obsession with it. On reflection, I guess that's because I always naturally felt that I owned all my goals, and that with enough work and effort, I would be able to find a path to achieve anything.

At least, I felt that way until the CEO changed, and I experienced that fateful out-of-control two years, eventually crashing to rock bottom. Understanding what I know now about Snyder's work, I can totally see why I lost all sense of hope. The CEO decided I wasn't her cup of tea, and no matter how hard I worked, I couldn't change her mind. So when it came to having hope for my career under her leadership, I felt I neither had the ability to control my career (agency), nor did I have the way to find successful pathways to getting my career on track (ability). That's not to say that I didn't keep trying to find successful pathways—the warrior princess in me never gives up—and eventually I came back into favour with her, but the career she believed I was capable of and my hopes for my own career were miles apart.

One of the darkest characteristics of that time was the lack of hope. It felt suffocating. A never-ending blackness. The elephant crushing my chest just would not get off, no matter how hard I pleaded with it to swiftly move along. Shame in stereo drowned out any Still Small Voice. I had low energy and no sense of purpose. As always, a good anthem was needed, and this time it was "Breathing" by Watershed:

So I hold on tighter
The losing fighter
You just keep breathing
Barely believing

You've taken from me
My hopes and my dreams[3]

As with most rock-bottom moments in life, it wasn't just caused by one thing—my professional woes. John and I had been trying for our second child for over a year when all of this began, and we were in the middle of one failed fertility treatment after the other. My body was so pumped full of hormones I would burst into tears at the most arbitrary point in the middle of a meeting. Me, the softest thing about me being my teeth, in tears? Needless to say, my all-male team learnt quickly when I was in the middle of a fertility cycle and would look wide-eyed at me, I think secretly wishing the hard-assed, bra-burning bitch would return!

By the time the IVF did work and I eventually fell pregnant, I had taken on the management of a R3bn business. Eight weeks into my pregnancy, I was admitted to hospital—an event that led to being bed-ridden for five months, on maternity leave for four months, and my job being given to someone else in my nine-month absence. I returned to work jobless, and with new-born twins, I had neither the headspace nor the physical energy to consider moving companies. I was stuck in a deep black groove. Hopeless.

So let's go back to that question: Why is it that we have lost the ability to dream?

We've all been so beaten down by life that dreaming feels like a waste of time. Before the rock bottom years, it never occurred to me that I wouldn't be CEO of a listed company. With hard work, I could achieve anything. What was amazing is how I believed I could never achieve that after rock bottom. I was the same human with the same experience and talent, but I had lost all hope—it felt like the CEO had the agency and the pathway, and I had no ability to make my dream happen.

But the power of dreaming an unconstrained dream has truly been revealed to me over these last two years since I started *Working Women's Wealth*. I first set the goal to teach one million women about living their Best Life and money before I died. I thought that that was one of those Big Hairy Audacious Goals that Jim Collins spoke about in his book *Built to Last*.[4] But my osteopath challenged me that it was, in fact, too limiting.

"What about two million? Why by the time you died? Why not in five years?"

It got me thinking, why not? So I set the goal to teach one million women by the time I was fifty. That left me seven years.

The thing is, the more I talk about the goal, the more public it becomes and the more doable it feels.

"This is Lisa Linfield, and her goal is to teach one million women about money" now doesn't feel as scary an introduction as it did in the beginning. Over a very short time, my goal has become part of my identity, part of my I *am* and I *can* statements so much so that I now believe that I *can* teach one million women about money.

That brings us back to Professor Locke and Professor Snyder's theories on goals—that they need to be specific, clear, and a big enough challenge to keep you motivated, and that you need to feel that you can personally own them and have the ability to direct their successful outcome.

I guess that's why with time, I don't have a doubt in my mind that I will achieve it. Because I own it, no one else does, and no one else is making me do this. And I know that I can find a way to make it happen—that through the books I will write, the talks I will give, and the courses I will teach, at some stage I will hit a million women.

But whilst that is my goal, it's not as big as my vision. When I give myself permission to dream, I'm in heaven with God, and He stands with me, looking over a huge, lush green valley in the most beautiful setting one could ever imagine. He zooms in and starts showing me the faces and telling me the stories of *all* the people impacted by my work. Not just the one million women—their children, husbands, or friends who have, in some way, had a better life because I stepped outside my comfort zone many, many times, just to reach my goal to teach them.

"Look what we did together," He says and gently squeezes my hand. "Thank you for being brave enough to step into the purpose I created for you, and thank you for using your gifts to the best of your ability." And as I see that picture, I cry. I always do!

My biggest inspiration story is of one of my all-time heroes, Sir Nicholas Winton. From 1938 to 1939, he saved the lives of 669 children from the Holocaust, organising and paying for seven trains to evacuate the children from Czechoslovakia before the war began and Hitler shut the boarders, closing the route through Germany to England. He kept quiet about it for fifty years, not even telling his wife, because he felt it was of no value. To cut an amazing story short, when she found a book in their attic detailing each child's journey fifty years later, she argued that it wasn't only his story but also the children's story, and they had a right to know the truth about their history.

And so unravelled a sequence of events that surfaced the story, a story that has impacted the more than 6,000 descendants of those children whose lives he saved. In a surprise organised by the BBC, he got to meet many of those children for the first time. When asked how, with no training or infrastructure, he paid the fifty-pound bond the government required to let them into the UK and personally organised a host family for each one of the children, he replied,

"I work on the motto that if something is not impossible, there must be a way of doing it." [5]

On my podcast, one of the guests I interviewed, Gloria Mitchell, explained a concept to me that truly blew me away. She has a remarkable story, encapsulated in the fact that she was homeless with no university degree at the age of twenty and went on to achieve a Stanford MBA and so much in her life. That small summary really doesn't do her justice in terms of the journey that she's been through, but it is very significant to add context to her thinking below.

The big Ah-Ha for me came in our discussion on the difference between elite performers and everybody else. "No one reaches the highest level of success by focusing on the probability of it; they focus on the possibility. Is it possible? And if it's possible, they figure out a way to make it happen."[6] Sir Nicholas Winton was living proof of that—if it is possible, there must be a way.

How many of us don't dream because we feel it's highly improbable that we could ever achieve our dreams? Either because we're so deeply stuck in our groove we can't see another way, or because we've failed before, or our inner critic or primary school teacher tells us that we'll never amount to anything, we believe we'll never be able to achieve *that*.

So I ask my "Brave to Be Free" course participants one clear question: **has someone in a similar or lesser circumstance ever achieved what you want to do?** And if they have, then know deeply with every fibre of your being that it is *possible* to achieve it—and focus on that.

You just need Professor Snyder's ingredients of hope: believe deeply that you can, and you'll find a way.

JOURNALING

I want you to dream in a totally unconstrained way. What does that mean?

Whenever you feel that logical part of your brain saying, "That's impossible," just shhhhhhhhh. Quieten it down. When you hear your inner critic saying, "You'll never be able to . . ." just shhhhh. Quieten it down. When you feel that this dream goes against what that good little girl in you *should* be doing, hush it up, buttercup.

This is the original La-La Land, a place where you can be and do whatever you want. Where you can choose to live wherever you want, choose to be with whomever you want, and choose to do the work that truly makes you feel happy—or not.

- What does it feel like to not have to worry about where money comes from?
- What does it feel like to spend time doing only what you are passionate about doing and only with the people you choose to be with?

- Who is with you? Where are you?
- What are you doing now that you would continue to do in La-La land?

Finally, summarise it into a clear goal.

The Journey

But as important as the vision is, the journey along the road to get there is just as important.

Why? Because we have *no* idea what will happen in life or whether the goal will be all we think it will be. Sometimes we reach a goal, and think, "Wow, this isn't as fun as I thought it would be." Having a clear vision of the journey along the way helps us to be open to enjoying every step of the goal and reduces the possibility of finding we've given so much of our life, only to end up in the wrong place.

If I'm honest with myself, and not spouting good-little girl reasons, the higher I went in corporate, the less I enjoyed it. I like doing and being, not sitting in meetings about meetings about a board meeting that's happening in three months' time. Or the fourteenth version of the budget pack recrafting meeting—when in fact they should have just said, "A hundred million is the target; find a way to make it happen."

Can you imagine if I hadn't listened to my gut, followed the sign-posts, and ended up where I thought I wanted to be? I think I would have been a miserable CEO of a big company, doing a good job but at the expense of my soul.

I'm nowhere near my goal of teaching a million women. But I don't think it matters if I do or don't ever reach it. The journey I am on currently far surpasses my wildest dreams.

I have a whole new energy, a new way of being as a result of this journey. When people I haven't seen in a while meet up with me, they say, "Goodness, Lis, you look different. What's going on?" I really have a spring in my step as a result of this new sense of purpose. I've loved new conversations at the dinner table with John as I share with him my latest learnings or who I'm meeting. My discussions with others are really different because they're very broad, focused on the big-picture issues of life, not who did what to whom in the corporate food chain. Life's about this amazing thing that I'm working on for this great and higher purpose.

Through my podcast episodes, I've met amazing human beings that I would never have met, let alone connected with on such a deep level. Just today I met another financial adviser who heard me speak about the philanthropy I do to teach domestic helpers about money. In Johannesburg for a day, he reached out to connect and shared his vision of helping others with the amazing financial knowledge our profession gives us. He's helping the poorest of the poor to set up their own businesses and teaching them the financial skills as they go.

Another part of my journey I'm grateful for is that I get to teach my kids by example about what it's like to pursue something you're passionate about. I work every single Saturday and many evenings, and my girls see it. But they also know that I have the flexibility to watch them at their swimming gala or take them to their ballet exam. I'm teaching them every single day about what it takes to pursue your passion, what it means to do something that matters, and to do something that you love doing.

But I'm also teaching them what it means to put your family first when it matters, to prioritise God, and the gift of flexibility and the ability to determine how your time is spent. They know that I get such great energy from it, and they also learn so much from our dinnertime conversations as I share my successes and my failures.

JOURNALING

- In La-La land, what does your journey to your dream look like?
- Who's learning with you? Who are you meeting?

- What conversations are you having? What conversations are you no longer having to have (either in your head or with your colleagues or partners)?
- Where are you going on this journey? Does it take you to new cities? Does it give you the flexibility to work from home or take vacations more often?
- What does a day, a week, and a month look like?

As you journal your vision and your journey to that vision, hush your objections along the way. Activate every single part of your brain—imagine what would it look like, feel like, smell like, and what would you see and hear.

Finally, summarise it into a clear journey.

Little-Known Secrets for Step-Change Success

14

Free Your Mind for the Best Chance of Success

Visiting La-la land is a powerful journey. To be in touch with the dreams that had gone rusty, the hopes that lifted your heart, and the sense of energy and invincibility that comes from shutting down Cruella de Vil . . . there is nothing quite like that.

But as freeing as it is, the big problem when we return to reality is the constant jabbering inside our head, the nagging reminders about how silly this idea is, how certain it is that we will never achieve it, and how stupid we are for even doing the exercise.

So that brings me to limiting beliefs: Cruella's back-up crew that sings the chorus of reasons why we can't achieve it. When it comes to limiting beliefs that stop us from living our Best Life, they generally tend to fall into three categories:

1. Beliefs about yourself
2. Beliefs about others
3. Beliefs about The World Out There.

I was recently working with a client who was considering taking a job offer overseas. Of all the countries in the world, this was where she wanted to live, and she had been wanting to leave South Africa for a long time. However, I listened to her go on for more than five minutes about how certain she was that she wouldn't enjoy living there, how unlikely it was that the people in the new company were going to be nice, and how, despite the job being good on paper, no job *ever* lives up to the expectations.

Honestly, I wanted to scream at her, "For Pete's sake, if you're so convinced at how awful it will be, don't go, but don't *ever* mention again how much you want to go live there and how you'll do anything to make it happen."

Her limiting belief chorus was reeling off every verse they knew about why she, the job, and the country would be awful in this opportunity. It was exhausting listening, and I knew that like all of us, she had just shared the tip of the iceberg of the chorus that was plaguing her every minute of the day as she considered this decision. As her dream was becoming a reality, Cruella was trying to keep her in the safety of the groove she knew, not the vision her little 50 bits of consciousness had been thinking about.

At the core of all these limiting beliefs are assumptions. And as the good saying goes, they truly are the mother of all fork-ups.

More often than not, assumptions are not true, and they block true thinking. Nancy Kline, in her powerful book *More Time to Think: The Power of Independent Thinking*, suggests the one way to remove limiting assumptions is to ask an incisive question.[1] The goal is to try and get our mind to replace incorrect assumptions that limit our life with true assumptions that unlock possibility and with our belief that we are able to find a journey to our goal, regardless of whatever roadblock we may be experiencing.

JOURNALING

As you did the exercise of unconstrained dreaming, those little buts and ifs and stupids started creeping in. Think carefully about the answer to this question and, as the answers start tumbling out, journal them as much as possible.

- What do I really believe about my ability to achieve this goal?

Write down everything you can think of—as many bullets as possible—without filtering, trying to get from Good Reasons to Real Reasons by asking Five Whiskeys and a Heineken or doing a Reverse

Thinking Stack. Then take time to look back over the answers—some will resonate more deeply than others, almost like that Still Small Voice says, "These are the Real Reasons for doubting myself."

- Choose three of them to journal further and ask yourself,
    » What am I assuming about [this dream] that makes me think I can't achieve it?
    » What else?

One of two things will happen to you. Either you will get that Ah-Ha moment where your Still Small Voice resonates with the answer, identifying it as the Real Reason you don't think that you can make this goal a reality; or you may need to sit with the list longer, asking yourself, "Which one of these is really stopping me?"

Then summarise your limiting beliefs into a list. For example:

- I believe that my husband will never agree to me going back to work.
- I believe that my kids will be less happy if I'm at work.
- I believe I don't have the willpower to lose 10 kgs (22lbs).
- I believe I will never find a partner who loves me for who I am.
- I believe I'll never get a promotion either in my existing company or another.
- I believe the only option available to me is having my mother live with me, because no one else can care for her like I can.

The challenge in life is that our thinking drives our behaviour. And as we know by now, most of our thinking is deeply embedded in our subconscious (those eleven million bits per second)—which is difficult to observe, let alone work out why we behave as we do. The good news is we know already how to do that—we go back to our Thinking Stack to find our deepest limiting beliefs.

Let's take an easily understandable example of money and work through it. If you are unable to make money, unable to hold onto your money, unable to invest money, unable to enjoy true financial freedom, the reason is *not* because you're doing something wrong—it's because you're thinking something wrong.

Let's say you're in the parking lot, politely waiting and indicating for a space, and just as you put yourself in gear to go into it, a Porsche SUV cuts in front and takes your place.

"You see, all rich people are idiots!" you yell out loud.

Now that is a beautiful moment to question your thinking and journal about it later. You could ask yourself two streams of questions:

Thinking Stream 1

"Why do I assume that people who drive Porsche SUVs are rich?" Don't just accept the answer "Because they are very expensive." Go through the Reverse Thinking Stack:

What causes us to feel like we do now?

1. **Trigger**—Porsche cuts me off.
2. Earliest **Event**—I remember my grandfather was driving me in his car in the parking lot and a big Mercedes cut him off. It was the first time I'd heard him swear like that. Actually, my dad, his son, did that often too. I interpreted it as a dislike for rich people who felt they owned the world.

What's going on below the surface?

3. **Assumptions** (the story I'm telling myself)—Porsche = rich.
4. **Feeling**—Anger that they think they can do exactly as they want, and if I dig to Real Reasons, jealousy that I'm still driving my tiny little car.
5. **Instinct**—Fight—I want to ram that car.

Then you need to question that limiting assumption.

6. Is it really true that people who drive expensive cars are wealthy?

In my experience as a financial adviser who gets to look behind the scenes, it's often the complete opposite. The more expensive the car and house, the more debt and less wealth a person often has. For me, expensive cars = paying for the bankers to go on holiday. Yes, the person may have a high income, but wealth is the assets that you have that generate the money for *you* to sit on the beach. Expensive cars eat money; they don't generate money. It does happen that people are wealthy enough to afford both the expensive car and have a huge amount of money invested—but most times, it isn't the case.

Thinking Stream 2

The second question I would ask is, "Why do I assume that all rich people are idiots?" In your life growing up, who was rich and an idiot, according to your parents? What experiences led you to know that? Then find examples of rich people who aren't idiots so that you can change your limiting belief.

You will *never* be wealthy, be able to hold onto money, be able to live the life you want if you believe that rich people are idiots. Your subconscious will just never let you do that to yourself—become an idiot—as it goes against everything you believe. It strives for congruency—the branches of the trees of our life can't be disconnected from the roots. Oranges can't grow from an apple tree. So your behaviour has to reflect your deepest thinking. As long as you think rich people are idiots, your money will keep disappearing.

In my own life, a vision that I struggled with involved owning my own business. When I was in first year university, the interest rates in South Africa shot up over 20 percent. My dad owned a manufacturing business and all the machines were financed, and like most people, he couldn't afford double the interest payments.

Since then, for me owning a business meant that you could lose everything. Not just losing a salary, you can lose *everything* you ever had. I remember clearly coming home from university and the computer that had all my essays and work for the year was gone—taken by the creditors. Of everything that happened through that period, that was the most impactful symbol of losing the business—they take everything, even your daughter's computer.

As you can imagine, leaving a large corporate salary to set up my own business has been a really deep journey with this assumption. Even being able to dream it required a lot of work. If I'm honest, it still slows my growth, since I'm scared to invest all-in in my business in case I jeopardise everything we've worked so hard to save.

So, is my assumption *always* correct? Does everyone who ever has their own business lose everything? No. Therefore I regularly store in my memory examples of people and types of businesses that *don't* result in losing your life savings.

Liberating Assumptions

Once you know what's stopping you and have reverse-engineered what caused you to think that, how you interpreted it, and what assumptions you're making, you need to reframe the limiting assumption into a liberating assumption. Nancy Kline has the best method for this that I have seen.

Let's say that your dream is to own your own bed-and-breakfast (BnB) on a beautiful beach, a business that would make enough money to keep you well sorted in your retirement.

But your Cruella de Vil says, "Don't be stupid—you will never have enough money saved up to buy it with your current salary and all the expenses you have now, and no one will ever come to your BnB."

When you deep dive it, the real issue is that your mum always spoke about having her own BnB but never managed to save enough for it. Therefore, your assumption is that they are very expensive and you too won't be able to save enough.

If the limiting assumption is you won't be able to save enough, then the liberating assumption is that you could find a pathway to save enough—either because you can cut your expenses or get more income from your current job, a new job, or a side hustle. You can also back up that assumption by dealing in facts—researching the cost of a house on a beach you could afford and how much you need to save to make it happen.

We then turn that into a liberating question—If you knew *[liberating assumption]*, then how would that change *[what you do now]*?

If you knew that *you would be able to find a way to save enough money for the BnB by the time you retire by creating more income from a side hustle*, then *what would you start today to make sure that happens*?

All of a sudden, you now have a liberating belief to replace your limiting belief. But something greater starts to happen in your brain.

Time for more brain science. I love the hacks that brain science gives us!

There's a tiny part of our brain called the Reticular Activating System whose job it is to evaluate opportunities and find solutions. If you were to imagine long time ago when food was starting to run scarce, and it was deeply worrying you—How would you feed your family? Where are you going to get food?—your brain would continuously be scanning the environment for opportunities for food. Even things that you might not have originally thought of in terms of food, like cockroaches or worms or any weird and wonderful flower.

For example, let's say you're a fisherman and you're on your boat, navigating the seas. The back of your brain is always thinking about what happens if a storm comes. What happens if something threatens me or endangers me? Your brain is always scanning—scanning for whether the weather is turning, the wind is changing directions, the time it's taking for the sky to becoming overcast, or if the swell is rising.

The Reticular Activating System is always scanning. It's like the powerful control centre for a missile—it locks on and goes for its target, finding whatever route it needs to take to follow it until BOOM! you hit it. It seeks out opportunities to fulfil what your subconscious is focused on in order to protect and provide for you. Once you're certain of something and it's clear and simple in your mind, then you will find it through this Reticular Activating System. But that's the key—it needs to be certain and simple.

But it is also what confirms our thinking. It looks for data that will confirm whatever our assumptions or deeply held beliefs are. It evaluates everything we see, hear, and think, sifts out unimportant babble, and holds on to the important stuff. It's why if you're buying a yellow Ford, you see yellow Fords everywhere.

But it's also why two people can be in the same conversation and hear totally different things. Because they seek out the words or phrases that totally re-enforce their viewpoint—and don't hear anything that might back the other person's point of view. It's the reason I need to take detailed minutes of financial meetings—because it's amazing how often I wonder if we were even in the same room, let alone part of the same conversation. Things on my client's mind get burnt into their recollection, and things on my mind get burnt into mine—and we can forget each other's pressing priorities.

Therefore, if you think you're never going to achieve something, your Reticular Activating System will scan all the data it comes across, picking out pieces that confirm that your subconscious is correct, that you will never achieve that.

But here's the good news: the Reticular Activating System must be told what to look for. What you spend your time thinking about is what it will focus on. The more you think about the future you want, the opportunity you need—somehow, magically, it will come. It truly isn't magic though, it's good old fashioned focus and a really great piece of brain science.

That magic only happens though when two conditions exist: **certainty and simplicity**. Often, if your goals are not coming to you, if your mind is not seeing those opportunities, it's because the goals are too complex. Your subconscious is still working to figure its way through the noise of the complexity, not focusing on creating those opportunities. As Professor Edwin Locke showed us, goals need to be specific and clear, certain and simple to be achieved—because that's what the Reticular Activation System needs.

If your limiting belief is that you'll never be able to save enough to buy the BnB, then no matter how much visioning you do and certainty you think you are creating, your brain will only show you why you can't do it. Or if you want to lose weight and your limiting belief is that for the rest of your life you will need to live off lettuce leaves, then it's guaranteed that you will never be able to stick to a diet—because nothing in your soul or body wants to live off lettuce leaves alone. In my money work, if you believe that wealthy people are idiots, believe me, your brain will not allow you to intentionally be an idiot, so you won't reach your goals.

It all comes down to understanding the Good Reasons your brain tells you when you're trying to motivate yourself with those fifty bits per second versus the Real Reasons your subconscious tells you why you won't be able to have what you want.

JOURNALING

Incisive questions for limiting beliefs and identity

Remember when we talked about something you tried to change on many occasions but couldn't? Pull out the Reverse Thinking Stack journals where you recorded your Identity Statements (I *can* or I *am*).

For example: I believe I *am* never going to lose weight because I believe that everyone in my family has always been fat. It's just the way it is.

Now change the limiting assumption into a liberating assumption question using the formula:

If you knew *[liberating assumption]* then how would that change *[what you do now]*?

So, if you knew that you had the power, discipline, and toolset available to reach your goal weight and stay there forever, then how would you change the way you ate and exercised now?

Then spend some time answering that question.

Reticular Activating System

With respect to the new liberating assumption above, what is *one thing* you can focus on to begin to create enough data that in fact your new liberating assumption is correct.

So, instead of focusing on an entire diet and exercise plan, focus on doing fifty squats every morning. That's it. One thing. Clear, concise, simple.

15

Rocket Fuel

So you have a big dream. It's an exciting challenge, but you know that you'll be able to find a way to make it possible because someone, somewhere, in the same or less fortunate circumstances has managed to achieve it. No matter how probable it is, you believe it is possible to achieve your dream. You can do it, and you know that with the lock on guidance system of your Reticular Activating System, you can find a pathway to make it happen. So you have hope. You've written the dream down, challenged every single assumption about why you can't make it and reaffirmed what is your true I *am* and I *can* identity statements around this, and then written a liberating question that has caused your brain to open up to the thousand options out there to make your dream happen.

Now what?

Now you need to understand deeply why you want to do this. I'm talking about the Real Reasons why *you* want to do it, not the Good Reasons The World Out There tells you why you should do it. Knowing your why is crucial because it will become the rocket fuel of your dream, the energy you'll need to get out of the groove you're in and take you to your goal, braking you free from your limiting beliefs and old ways of 'doing things.'

You'll need this rocket fuel because there will be tough times. You will need to dig deep to that place inside you that knows what it is that you are hoping to achieve and why. And trust me, if you're trying to dig deep based on a cheesy World Out There why, it will never give you the grit to keep going.

I love the work of Angela Duckworth. She wanted to know why the US Military Academy at West Point could run all the best tests available to select the best candidates, yet they still suffered significant drop out in the "Beast Barracks"—the notorious six-week basic training program designed to push candidates to their limit, physically and mentally.

After 11,258 candidates were assessed over a ten-year period—testing (i) cognitive mental ability (such as the ability learn, problem solve, plan, and reason), (ii) physical ability, and (iii) grit—Angela and her team proved that grit was the strongest determinant of success. Grit, they defined, was the "passion *and* perseverance for long-term goals of personal significance."[1]

Living your Best Life is a long-term goal of personal significance. And without question, there are going to be many times when you want to give up in favour of comfort and will need to persevere if you are to achieve it.

It echoes Rick Snyder's work on hope being connected with your agency (belief you can) *and* your ability to find a pathway. What you believe *and* what you do.

It's not enough to feel deeply the passion for your dream and believe deeply that you can achieve it. You need to be able to persevere, to keep going, and to have the emotional strength to search for and find a path around the obstacles. And if that fails, you need the diligence to find that next path, and the next-next path, until you reach that goal. It's that ability to dig deep, clench your teeth, and keep going when everything inside you wants to give up and The World Out There tells you, "It's OK. Anyone in your position both could and should give up."

You must have an exceptionally strong reason why, one that you believe with every cell in your body—the Real Reason you want to live your Best Life.

Interestingly, Angela also found that for many, the most effective whys are a reason outside yourself—the cadette wanting to get through basic training to see a child or a loved one or the cadette not wanting to face the faces of all those people who told him he would screw up and drop out. For many of the clients in my business, a big external why they want to sort out their retirement saving is that they refuse to be a financial burden on their children. For some, it's to prove people wrong.

Starting my businesses had many whys. 'Out there' reasons:

- The desire to change the direction of someone's life, like I had the opportunity to do with Mary. I always say that helping someone is the best form of natural high you can ever get—it lifts your soul heavenward, makes you hum, and energises your whole day.
- To build something meaningful that could change the world.
- The obedience in answering the call I believe God gave me to remove the heavy burden of worry that chains His daughters and weighs them down.

'Other based' reasons:

- The flexibility I craved to be able to *both* be present in my little girls' life *and* have a meaningful career.

My reasons:

- The desire to be the master of my own destiny, to control my career and not be at the whim of a changing CEO or organisational restructure. I had a deep sense that there was a gap between my potential and what I was able to achieve in a corporate.
- The fear of being force-retired at age sixty by a company when I knew I would still want to work, still contribute. Again, I feared someone else determining my life, my work, my success.

As my businesses have grown and my thinking matured, my whys to make these businesses a success have evolved:

- The fear of shame is a big why I use to my advantage—I don't want to fail in my publicly stated goal of teaching a million women about money.

- The people I've met on my journey have become a big why—
they point toward the people I want to and will meet going
forward. I want my life to be surrounded by more of these
amazing humans.
- The determination to pay back every cent I've borrowed from
John and my savings to start my businesses.
- The opportunity to craft a life I dream of—an international
speaking career that takes me to amazing places around the
world; the flexibility of a location-independent business that
allows me to visit my children wherever they are in the world.
- The commitment to give people good financial advice that
puts their needs first and helps them to live independently in
their retirement. The retirement crisis burns my soul in a way
I can only imagine climate change burns Greta Thunberg's
soul. I have a sense of panic from which springs an almost
evangelical need to tell the whole world that a train is about to
crash into them and if they don't change their behaviour now,
they will condemn the future generations to paying for their
debts, their lifestyle. I'm motivated both by the shame I feel
that so many in my profession give such awful advice and a
deep desire to change my profession for the best.

I don't believe in only one why. And the whys you start with will
evolve as you take your first brave step—and those other whys will step
in to add energy to your path. Life's challenges are varied, and at different times, you'll need different whys to pull you through. When I'm
putting in way too many hours, I remind myself that one of my whys
for doing this is to spend more time with my family, not less. I then
force myself to pull back.

When I see a fifty-six-year-old woman whose life savings has grown
just 1 percent per year since she was in her twenties because some idiot
took extortionate fees over those thirty years and only saw her once that
fateful day in her twenties—that anger becomes my rocket fuel, triggering my why to get quality financial advice into the hands of the many.

When I meet with men who are two months before sixty or
two months after, and they feel empty of purpose and angry at their

company for forcing them to stop work when they feel they still have so much to offer—that's when the why of flexibility and control over my future is rocket fuelled and I am deeply grateful that I can determine my own path.

If your whys aren't strong enough to pull you through the tough times, then you must really stop and think to yourself, "Am I being honest with myself when it comes to this goal? How badly do I want it?"

Figuring Out Your Why Not

I am so sugar intolerant, it's scary. As I write this, I'm suffering the aftereffects of the ice cream and gluten-free shortbread that I ate yesterday—the pressure in my sinuses, the feeling of the elephant sitting on my head, the lethargy that makes me want to curl up into a ball.

When I go through my Reverse Thinking Stack, I know why I can't give it up. I went on my first diet at ten years old. I remember clearly going to Weigh-Less—the South African equivalent of Weight Watchers—and weighing in, confessing my sins, being measured. I remember not eating nice things when my friends were, feeling deprived. Being on and off diet was a feature of my life until I hit twenty-five, and with each diet I only got fatter.

I know the real reason I can't give up sugar is that I'm terrified of a 'boring' life of lettuce leaves and deprivation. I hate that feeling of missing out on the nice things. But, my biggest trigger for sugar is not emotions but tiredness. Come 4 p.m., I'm desperate for the rush of sugar, and that goes on until I go to bed. Before 4 p.m., I really couldn't care less.

The fact that I haven't been able to give up sugar—and the fact that I keep saying, "From Monday I will"—proves that my Real Reasons for wanting to give it up (my whys) are not strong enough, not top of mind enough, to say no yet. To be honest, those whys are not as strong as the whys of surviving the day, trying to achieve all I'm working on at the moment—being a mother of three, owner of three businesses, daughter, friend, author, creator of three courses in different stages, and the list goes on.

If I'm honest, my passion to achieve those goals is far more important to me than not eating sugar. And whilst I know intellectually that it would be easier to achieve them if I felt on top of my game health-wise, I also know that when I just need a little endorphin and energy boost, I reach for the ice cream or chocolate.

So between the two of us, the answer to "How badly do you want it now?" has got to be "not badly enough." It just feels like one more willpower-draining, brain-energy-sapping straw that will break this camel's back when she's only just holding up under the weight of it all some days!

My ability to stick to my twice-weekly gym session is deeply rooted in how rock bottom felt when I never had the strength to walk up a flight of stairs after my pregnancy with the twins. How desperate it was to not be strong enough to run after my little ones. It's rooted in the deep fear of sitting on a couch in my retirement versus the dream of an active retirement, cycling through France, walking the cherry blossoms in Japan, climbing to Machu Pichu. That why of 'strength to enable me to live life to its fullest,' and the external accountability of paying a trainer is enough to get me there consistently. But I make sure I do it in the morning when my willpower is still high, because my like-lihood of cancelling goes way up in the evening when my energy drops!

That's a brain science point you want to note. You have two hours of optimal frontal lobe processing time. That means that you need to make sure those tough things that do need willpower get done in the morning. It's one of the reasons I find it so hard to resist sugar after 4 p.m.—my frontal lobe has no strength against the energy low!

When you look at your own whys, keep pushing through them to find the real reason. Is this really the reason? Jot down as many as you can think of and think deeply on the events that trigger them. I call those "Memory Photographs" and consciously file them to remind me why I need to act. The realisation that I had only managed to see one of Jess's netball matches in a season was a deeply motivating why for flexibility; it reminds me why I never want to be in that position again. It's a Memory Photograph, filled with shame and feeling. The humiliation of returning to work with no meaningful job, and the feeling of worthlessness, being tossed aside—that Memory Photograph is a huge why for never letting someone else dictate my success, for the agency of choosing my own pathway in life. And as mentioned, struggling to walk up the stairs in my house after my pregnancy with the twins— why I exercise. All those deeply ingrained Memory Photographs get pulled up whenever I want to quit.

As powerful as your why is, so is your *why not.*

You discover your why not by asking yourself the question, "If I don't make this change, what will my life look like in ten years' time?"

When I decided to start my own business, my wonderful boss Saks and I built a plan. I gave him six months' notice when I wanted to leave my full-time job, and then we had a plan for me to work half-day for a year afterward whilst I started setting up the business.

On the last day of my formal full-time employment, I went to see our HR Director, Unati, for that formal paperwork stuff. It's scary, taking that final step of commitment. You doubt yourself, and Cruella steps in in a big way. "What are you doing? You're such an idiot to give up a successful career and all that money! You will never make this a success—you're not an entrepreneur and never will be. Don't be stupid. Stupid, stupid, stupid."

On the desk she had a pack of cards, and my curiosity got the better of me.

"What are these cards, Unati?"

"They're tarot cards for HR people!" she said in her usual light-hearted way. Now my curiosity was piqued.

"Tarot cards?"

"Yes. Shuffle them, pick three, and turn them over and read them, and one will stand out for you."

So, I shuffled them, picked three, and turned them over. They were coaching questions.

I can't remember what two of them said, but the one that stood out for me was the question, "What will you think about this decision in ten years' time?" And the Ah-Ha struck like a lightning bolt. I knew the answer without a shadow of a doubt. I knew I'd feel so grateful that I had the guts to take the step. To shut Cruella up and tell her to flock off. To take the plunge, step aside, and this time, intentionally swap my office for a hot desk.

A year later I found myself in Unati's office again. This time I was handing in my access card and laptop for good as I finished my year of half-day. Again, Cruella was going mad on how stupid and useless I was, giving up my safety net and my 'in' back into the corporate world.

Out of the corner of my eye I saw that pack of cards. I took them out the box, shuffled them, and reminded Unati of the cards I got this time a year ago.

When I chose my three cards and flipped them over, right in the middle was the exact same card out of more than fifty possibilities: "What will you think about this decision in ten years' time?"

My spirit soared, and I knew for sure that that was Cruella's last chance on this topic. I was done. No more corporate world. No more job. The next day I sat at my desk in my home office, a free woman. The opposite rang so true in my ears. What will you think about this in ten years' time if you *don't* make this decision?

When I do this question with the people on my "Brave to Be Free" course, it amazes me how powerful it is for them to imagine how their life will be if they don't achieve their goal. The realisation is that 'doing nothing' always results in more of the same of today but without the hope of life ever being something different. It's like today but way worse. Not only is there the darkness of no hope, but they're older with less energy and less time to create new pathways.

When I went a whole netball season and only saw Jess play once, I looked forward and saw something worse. When my twins grew up, I'd need to say to my girls that I could watch one of their netball matches every three years. For me personally, that was just not acceptable— I knew the guilt and the longing to share their journey through life meant I wanted to be there. I wanted to see each of them play as often as I could.

Knowing this has helped lift me up on many occasions when I messed up or things didn't go my way, kept me moving forward and spurred my energy in those early days when clients were few, expenses high, and the possibility of this working out was low.

Getting clear on your whys and why nots are your cornerstone of easy access to Rocket Fuel.

JOURNALING

Take the time now to jot down all the Good Reasons and the Real Reasons as to why you want to achieve your goal, change your path, and achieve your Best Life. For each of them, pause and think of a Memory Photograph filled with feeling that you can call on in times of need. Write that down in clear detail.

Then, imagine yourself in ten to twenty years. You're older, and a lot less energetic, and your brain is not as talented as it used to be. Maybe your kids and grandkids are or aren't around. This change you know you need to make now still hasn't been made. And your current trajectory is way worse. You may be way heavier, or more unfit; you may have a worse boss and moved from going sideways to going downward in the food chain; your marriage may have ended in divorce. Describe that scene in great detail of what you see, the words they say, how it feels.

Then, summarise and write down your why nots. What happens if you don't make the change you know you need to make to live your Best Life?

16

Shortcuts to Power

I'm a big fan of shortcuts—like Suitcase Phrases to quickly and unemotionally diffuse a potentially defensive and triggering situation or Memory Photographs to quickly remind me why I need to persevere.

When I'm grumpy and need a time out, I tell John, "I'm going for a long bath," which essentially means "Step away from the vehicle, it's about to explode—give me space, and know there is *no* good reason to interrupt me and my bath unless it's to silently bring me a refill of coffee (in the morning) or more gin and tonic (at night) or chocolate (any time). And if you do that, leopard-crawl in so I don't see you, lift the arm up around the bath to provide the refreshment, and leopard crawl back out—do *not* say a word!" In that one Suitcase Phrase, "I'm going for a long bath" comes years of understanding that doesn't need to be spoken into words.

Rewiring the brain for shortcuts to power seems to me like a good thing to do.

By changing your brain, you get to short-circuit some of the hard work necessary to rewrite limiting beliefs, change identity statements, and open yourself up to new possibilities. The brain needs energy efficiency, since it's the largest energy-user in our body. As a result, it's truly come up with a nifty way to do that for thoughts and actions we repeat often: the nerves that fire together, wire together. Instead of the nerves having to use a lot of energy to transmit from one to the other every single time, they start developing structural changes that 'wire' them together.

Nerves That Fire Together, Wire Together

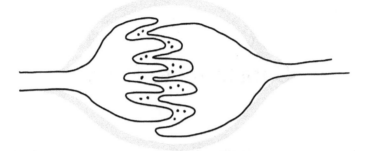

The first time we ever do something, the little neurons of the brain connect and use energy to make that connection, stimulating the little neurotransmitters activity to help the signal move from one to the other. It's why it takes us so much energy to learn new things. But the more we use those connections, the easier that little energy jump from the one nerve to the next becomes. Once we do it many, many times, our brain starts to 'hardwire' that connection. It builds a 'sheath' over the two nerves so that transmission can go quickly. It's a little like the reason why we have insulation on any of our electrical wiring—it helps the signal to go quicker and stops energy leakage.

We can short cut the process of creating new habits by deeply imagining the doing of the new habit with every part of our body—the pictures in our mind, the words out loud, the emotions we would feel, the colours we would see, and the right outcome we would know with every fibre in us we'll achieve.

But that sounds wishy washy. If we use the power of imagination, does our brain create these habits, and how strong are they? Well, think about your last nightmare. Our brain doesn't always know the difference between a real threat and something that happens in the subconscious. When we're having a nightmare, our brain perceives the threat as if it were happening in real life and initiates all the physical flight and fight responses in us. If we wake up from a nightmare, often we're sweating, we've kicked off our sheets, or we've physically acted out in response to this thing that's happening just in our brain—like shaking our partner. It always amazes me how angry I can feel against poor John after he's done something wrong in a dream.

When you have that Ah-Ha moment and suddenly shift your belief and thinking, it's powerful, exhilarating, energetic. You feel like the clouds have parted, and you have such clarity. But, like the paths and grooves we were discussing earlier in the book, thinking patterns that have been hard-wired together for so long are *way* more powerful than our new burst of energy thinking. Over time that clarity disappears and with it goes the energy, and before long you're back where you started.

Therefore, we need to rewire our brains. We need to be consistently reinforcing those new ways of thinking, making those nerves fire together so often that over time those thinking patterns will wire together. We're trying to repeat that thinking enough to move it from a conscious thought to the unconscious, the roots of the tree that drive our behaviour. We're trying to leverage the power of the eleven million bits per second rather than squeeze out the energy of the fifty bits per second in the hope that it will change our hard-wired habits.

Here's the thing: The National Science Foundation estimated you have between 12,000–60,000 thoughts per day. Other researchers say 70,000, some say 50,000. Regardless of how many there are exactly, there are a lot. The challenge is most of them are negative and a repetition of the previous day's thoughts. You are always in conversation with yourself—about yourself, about others, and about The World Out There (remind you of beliefs?).

Leveraging the Brain Science

Here's your choice: you can keep re-enforcing negative thoughts or use some of those 50,000 thoughts to dramatically change your life.

Let's go back to that goal—that unconstrained, detailed, emotion-filled dream of the life you want to lead. Pull it up in your brain with every sense that you have—experience it like you're living it right now using the same power of imagery and emotion that we have when we have a nightmare. Got it? Right.

Then get out those whys and why nots—the real ones, not the ones you think you should have. Get out all those little Memory Photographs. We're going to condense them into a shortcut, another form of Suitcase Phrase, a little thing that can trigger a waterfall of energy to wash over you when you need it most.

I've tried many forms of affirmations over my life. I started under the guidance of The Pacific Institute with affirmations that were present tense, emotive, and vivid. The one I remember most clearly (because it was at a time when I was struggling with my health and trying to become pregnant) was "I love my strong, lean, Demi Moore body that gives me the energy I need to live my Best Life." It was then that I learnt about the Suitcase Picture, and I chose one of Demi Moore doing the one-armed push-up in *G.I. Jane*. For me, that was the symbol of strength, and I imagined myself being able to do this.

But the problem I've found with those affirmations is that fundamentally, many times they're a lie. I know at the time I don't have a strong, lean, Demi Moore body that I love, and even after over seven years at gym, I've never done a one-armed push-up ever! So I sense myself resisting it with everything inside me. I've progressed greatly from my three kneeling push-ups to whipping out a whole bunch of men's push-ups, but there's no zero body fat G.I. Jane lurking in this body!

My "Everyday Shortcuts to Power" are a mixture of all the work we have done and the principles of both Professor Locke and Professor Snyder. They are specific and clear; they are a challenge to reach; I believe I own them; and I will succeed in making them happen because there are multiple pathways open to me to achieve this goal that I can and will use. And I always summarise them with a Suitcase Picture I can doodle anytime and anywhere.

Everything I say in my affirmations is based on Real Reasons, not Good Reasons, and is based on a 'pass mark' of 50 percent of evidence.

Everyday Shortcuts to Power

1. Affirm it's **possible**. If someone, somewhere, in a similar or less fortunate position *can* do it, so can you.
2. Affirm your **identity statements** needed to underpin this goal (who I *am* and what I *can* do). Here you need to focus on the identity statements that you have done over 50 percent of the time (*not* perfection—50 percent is the pass mark).
3. Focus on the elements of **hope** and **goal setting**. Remind yourself,
    a. you *can* find pathways to make this goal happen,
    b. you have done hard things, and
    c. you have the passion and perseverance of grit.
4. Focus on **pre-visioning** what you will do to make it through the tough times to come (guaranteed) with any goal worth achieving
5. Ask **liberating assumption questions** that open your Reticular Activating System to find new possibilities and pathways that are clear and concise, that you can own, and that then create hope.
6. Draw a **Suitcase Picture** that sums up your dream. When you doodle it or imagine it, every feeling of success, of what this means to you, of your why comes pouring in.

As an example, let's take my dream to help one million women live their Best Life and be in control their money and use that dream to build up an affirmation using everything we've learnt so far.

Affirmation:

> *I know that there are people who have come from harder circumstances than I have, who have been able to achieve goals far bigger than teaching one million people. It is therefore totally possible for me to achieve my goal to help one million women live their Best Life and be in control of their money.*

Let's pause on it—there is nothing Cruella can argue with in that statement, no lies, no exaggeration. And it's in the present tense.

I AM able to teach one million women as I have the knowledge
I need and can source the people or skills I'm missing, and I
CAN teach a million women about money by the time I am 50.

This sentence is not only cementing my goal as part of **my identity**, it is also specific, clear, a challenge to reach, and in full ownership of my goal (agency).

There are many pathways to achieving this goal, and with God
leading the way, I will keep getting up and stepping into the
arena when life knocks me down; accepting that that's life's way
of sharpening my sword, building my strength, and enabling
me to find next-level ways to reach my goal.

This focuses on **pathways, on the perseverance of grit, and on pre-visioning** when the going gets tough (more on that later).

With God's help I will build a successful international speaking
career, author many books, host my own weekend seminars,
and build powerful training courses that all change lives.
Whatever comes my way, I know that with God's help I will be
able to get through it and another door will open.

My current **Liberating Assumption Question** is:

If you knew that every step you took in your sales and
marketing efforts would ultimately lead you to the success you
will have, what would you do differently?

They key, as always, is to write it down and with it create the **Suitcase Picture** that you can doodle, imagine in your head, and draw on at any time.

The Suitcase Picture

My Suitcase Picture is of a day in the future at a beautiful old theatre like the Royal Albert Hall in London, when I fill every one of the 5,554 seats and can see the faces of the many people whose lives I'm changing. When I'm doodling, I doodle that.

The thing about your subconscious, about changing your identity or triggering the Reticular Activating System, about achieving your goals, is that it loves the constant repetition of a specific, clear phrase or goal. So remind yourself every time you brush your teeth, every time you shower, whenever you drive, when you go to bed at night. But the change is best effected by using as many parts of your brain as you can at once—your emotions, your visualisation, the sounds you hear, the sights you see.

Keep writing and repeating it, keep drawing and doodling it, keep imagining it for a minimum of sixty-six days to change the habit. And journal the changes—those moments you realise you're starting to deeply believe it and that it is becoming part of your identity. At different times, I use different pieces of the long-form. Many times a day, I will say "I am going to teach a million women about money." At the moment, I'm struggling putting myself out there, and so ask myself the liberating question, "If you knew that every step you took in your sales and marketing efforts would ultimately lead you to the success you will have, what would you do differently?"

Music

Another shortcut I use is music. We all have songs that deeply resonate with us. When we put them on at full blast and scream the words from the bottom of our tummy as we fly down the highway, we feel we will take off.

I remember once feeling so beaten up by life, so unable to get up off the floor of the arena, so desperate to just give up and stay down. It was then that an amazing woman gave me a piece of homework that I thought was odd at the time. She told me to make a playlist of songs that lifted me from deep in my tummy, songs that pulled my heart out of ground and made it soar. And so I did, and it worked. In fact, I now have three playlists, and there are many times when those songs and their words connect to that Still Small Voice inside me and encourage me—rise up. March to the beat *you* drum, not the beat The World Out There says you should. And most of all, you were made for so much more.

As I mentioned earlier, my current anthem is "This is Me" by Kesha. When I listen to it, I'm in the Albert Hall, and it's packed with all those women. Like in a movie, the scene slows in time as I walk boldly out on stage with this song as the background music. I look out and just see the sea of faces looking at me. I pause and take it in—this is years of work to get to this stage, years of rejection, tiredness, heart-breaking moments, picking myself up off the floor.

As the song plays and the chorus rises faster, the words come out my belly, and every battle and fear leaves my body. The audience is clapping, welcoming me on stage, smiling at me. It's the time I see that there are more for me than there are against me. I look out into the faces of the women God has given me, and I just know the battle was worth it, because when my message does come out, God will use it to transform their hearts and change the path of their life.

By the time the song ends, every cell in my body believes my journey will get me to the Royal Albert Hall. That teaching one million women is completely doable. And that in that journey, I will find myself, the real me, the person God created—and not the bullshit I've let the world beat me into the ground about. As the song says, I am glorious. Not for anything I've done, but because God made me.

Find your song, friend, and let it seep into every cell.

JOURNALING

Create your affirmation from all your journaling to date, using mine as a framework. You can download the Everyday Shortcuts to Power framework at www.LisaLinfield.com/DeepGroovesDownload.

- Affirm it is possible—has someone, somewhere, in the same or lesser circumstances achieved something similar to what you want to do?
- Write your short, sharp identity statement, based on more than 50 percent success rate of actual behaviour.
- Write down the goal and affirm your ability to do hard things and create the pathways needed to persevere when things get tough.
- What clear and concise questions can you ask to affirm your liberating assumptions?
- Draw a picture that captures every single element of your dream—especially its emotion.
- Find a song that takes you there . . .

17

The Force Is Strong,
So Be Prepared

Never underestimate the powerful team of The World Out There, the pulling force of your Deep Grooves, and the viciousness of your personal Cruella de Vil. Together, it is in their interests to prove you wrong, to keep you safely as you were, to not let you change the status quo. Why?

Even those people who really love you and really want the best for you look at your life through their lens. If they have been burnt by being in corporate, they will think you're nuts to leave your life of entrepreneurship and join the corporate. If they personally could never imagine life without the big paycheck from banking or consulting—that paycheck represents their status, their safety, and their physical and emotional security—then they'll strongly advise you against leaving corporate. They will struggle to understand that giving that up is worth it—even if the price they pay by staying is their happiness.

For some in The World Out There, your choices represent a threat to their comfort. They believe the stories they tell themselves to justify staying in their groove—that there's no possible way to change, that this is only the next ten years you should stick it out for and then things will change. Your challenging that by changing grooves threatens that story, even when it has absolutely nothing to do with them.

My mum and I had been talking about going to see the Northern Lights for ages. One day, I was sent the itinerary and told to put my money where my mouth was! At that stage, I had just started my business, and financially, it was too much of a stretch. With a deep tear in my heart, I declined. At the last minute, a plan was made, and I joined her on a once-in-a-lifetime, bucket-list experience.

It didn't disappoint.

The trip up the Norwegian coast in a ship through the fjords was just magical, stopping past historic coastal towns each day to experience its beauty. As we went inland, we were blessed by a truly unbelievable experience of an electromagnetic shower. You get to see the Northern Lights on steroids! We were on our night-time snowmobile safari, hunting the lights in a remote lake and forest on a clear night (in itself a rarity over our trip). That night the sky looked like a child's lava lamp with blues, greens, and pinks dancing in the night, and no photo in the world could ever do that amazing experience justice.

The following day we both manned husky sleds, jumping off and pushing the sled up the riverbanks, desperately trying to keep up with three seriously fit huskies! As we levelled out on the fjord, the pleasure of the piercing silence, the pastel colours of the sun rising and setting were broken only by the panting and excitedness of the huskies, so happy to be racing in sync across the frozen fjords. The next day we finished our holiday with the overwhelming uniqueness of sleeping in the Ice Hotel at negative five degrees Celsius (way below freezing!).

To say I came back deeply energised is an understatement. The sacrifices I made to do that trip felt insignificant compared to the joy of sharing such a unique experience with my mum.

When I returned, another mum stopped me in the car park at school and, having glossed through small talk, started the next sentence with, "I just think I should give you some feedback . . ." Whenever someone says that or "Because I'm your friend I think I need to tell you . . .," everything inside my body clenches up, knowing what's coming next.

When it's coming from someone in the cheap seats in the arena, that's usually a sign that their self-justification onslaught is about to begin—and that it's not feedback intended to build you up from someone fighting in the arena with you.

What I'd love to do is summon every brave bone in my body and respond, "That's kind, but you don't need to burden yourself with giving me feedback," and walk right off before they start. But the people-pleaser in me is never brave enough to say that, so I have to paste a fake smile on my face while I imagine zipping her lips shut.

Anyway, she went on to tell me that she thought I should be more sensitive in my personal posts—that some people, like her, cannot afford to go to the Northern Lights. As she was justifying her position, her lips not even stopping to breathe, I looked over her shoulder at the new, expensive car she was leaning on and did a mental maths sum. At *best*, just the interest for that year's car payment was at least one-and-a-half times, probably double, the cost of my trip. That's before we even think about the cost of the car itself. I, on the other hand, drive an old, little, fully paid-off Honda Jazz.

My choice in life is to spend my money on experiences, relationships, living life to its fullest.

The World Out There will always criticise your choices because they are trying to justify theirs. My choice isn't right. Nor is it wrong. It's just my choice. And neither is hers right or wrong. For her, changing her car every five years is what she does. For us, we drive them till it's no longer safe—or it gets stolen, as is often the case in South Africa.

Whilst these are more overt examples of the resistance to your decisions or change, the hardest resistance is the everyday choices. I'm always amazed how people resist someone else's decision not to drink or not to have desert. "Go on, just have one . . . It's no fun when you don't drink," or "It's just one ice cream, it won't kill you." These self-justifications are cruel for a human who is using up every last ounce of willpower to stick to their promise to themselves—to lose weight, to cut down on alcohol, to support their functioning alcoholic husband through 'dry January.' We all have no idea what goes on inside the mind of another—and why on earth do they need you to drink to make them feel OK about the fact they are?

The Journey Four

It brings me to some practical guidance on supporting life's big shifts—so you have the strength to resist the force that pulls you back into the Deep Grooves. On this journey you need four people to walk this road with you: a mentor, a mentorship group, a friend, and an accountability partner.

The Mentor

One of the liberating mind shifts I've made is a result of interviewing many amazing women on my podcast. When I ask them who their mentors are, so many have mentioned people who have authored books on the area they're wanting to change, people who have podcasts, or blog posts, or videos that encourage and support them on their journey. Gone is the notion of the old-fashioned corporate mentor who helps you climb the ladder.

For every new thing I do or change I want to make, I find a virtual mentor. When I wanted to start a podcast, I bought Pat Flynn's course and learnt from him. I followed his podcasts and soaked up everything I could. When I wanted to launch my first course, I bought Amy Porterfield's course and listened to her podcast. And when I wanted to learn how to sell, I bought Russell Brunsen's courses and books.

The Mentorship Group

With each of these courses came closed online communities where I found like-minded people who were a few steps ahead, at the same place, and a few steps behind in the new groove I wanted to embed in my life. Normal, everyday humans with a dream like mine. And with each obstacle, I would reach out, and someone would answer my question and help me think through my options. When someone needed help that I could give, I freely shared, making me feel part of a tribe on a mission.

They say your mindset and attitude reflect the average of the five people you spend your time with. If those are people who think what you're doing is impossible, then you'll never get it done. When I launched my podcast, the South African podcast scene was tiny, in its infancy. No one had a clue what a podcast was or why on earth someone would even consider making one—especially if you weren't a radio presenter.

But because my time was spent online with people who had the same challenges and similar visions as I did, it felt completely doable and normal. For that part of my life, these people helped me create a new podcasting groove that now feels natural and is now understood by the people who originally thought I was nuts. I feel it's so important that you have everyday humans who are walking the road just like you to call on. I am by *no* means a groupie type of person, but I find tremendous support in fit-for-purpose groups of like-minded people—for short periods of time—who actually know what you're going through and are warriors in the arena with you every day.

Whether it be fertility, cancer, starting a new business, fixing your health, doing an Ironman, changing professions—find a group of people who have walked the journey, even if you just listen. Two people can say the exact same thing to you, but the one who is or has walked in your shoes—their advice will be gold.

I'm not saying you need to dump your friends and family; you've just got to learn who to talk to about what. My podcast group is where I share my podcast successes and struggles; my book writing group is where I share the details of this journey. The others around me in my everyday life know I'm writing a book, or know I'm podcasting, but the support of those in my group spans both technical and moral support—and their successes inspire me.

The Friend

That brings me to the third "person" you need: one friend who will understand your journey.

I've come to learn that whatever tough or great thing I'm going through in life, God will always draw one human alongside me to handle the journey in a meaningful way. When I was young, I believed the crap that The World Out There told you that your best friends or your partner should be 'the one' that walked every journey with you— these were your soul mates, and that's what they did, didn't they?

Looking back on my own journey and watching other people's journeys, I've come to see how hurtful those fairy tales, movies, and teenage stories are in the expectations they create. No one human can *ever* be your everything. That is just way too much pressure for anyone.

I learned this for myself during my pregnancy with the twins. After a *very* long, heart-breaking journey with infertility, we got the news late December 2010 that this IVF round was in fact successful—doubly successful, as both embryos had taken. Within a week the nausea had made way for full on Hyperemesis. With Jess, my first daughter, I was ill until I stopped breastfeeding, almost every day for over forty-five weeks. Not just first three-month nausea: full-on vomiting until I stopped breastfeeding. The twins made that look like a walk in the park.

By February I had my first hospitalisation. I'd woken up in the middle of the night bleeding. I called to John, and the sheer scale of it had us both sobbing our hearts out, convinced we had lost these precious angels we had struggled so hard to have. The only reason we even bothered going to hospital was the remote possibility that we may have lost only one but could still have one left. To our relief, the result of many tests showed that it was a torn placenta from the sheer abdominal pressure of being sick so much. They hospitalised me and gave me a drip of medicine that allowed for seventy-two hours of not being ill, enough time to start the healing process.

That was the start of many hospital visits and five months on and off in bed. A suspected brain tumour following three weeks of a migraine kept me under the bed covers. Premature labour at thirty-two weeks saw me hospitalised over the time my grandmother and closest friend died. And weeks of less dramatic moments were spent lying on the tiles next to the toilet. Despite birthing two healthy baby girls, I lost

15kgs (33 lbs) whilst I was pregnant and looked like a skeleton who had swallowed a beach ball.

Many people asked me if I read a ton of books and watched every movie and series ever made while I was sick. I wish I had been so lucky to have had the energy to read or watch TV. A good day was staring, mind blank, watching the weaver birds build their nests. A normal day was spent begging God to stop the nausea, thanking Him for the vomit that eased it, and waiting for the room to stop spinning whilst loving the coolness of the bathroom floor. At the back of my mind every single minute was the fear that all of this and my inability to eat were in fact hurting my babies, and like many twins, they would be born prematurely and might not survive.

Through that period, God bought me Yolande. She had been in my extended team structure at work briefly and had been diagnosed with cancer at a similar time. Despite never being close friends before being bed ridden, she became my pillar of support (and I hers) for that season in our lives. Long-term illness is so difficult for healthy people to understand—and they struggle with real empathy, the kind that is happy to sit in the room, say nothing, and read a magazine whilst you lie there.

In answer to the question, "How are you?" I chose honesty, and my friends struggled hearing that every day was shit. Some brutal, some less brutal. But all shit. To be fair, if I'd never been through that, I also would have stopped asking and stopped visiting. Yolande chose that stiff-upper-lip, everything-is-fine version. Her friends got really mad with her for lying and not being honest. We both decided our approach clearly didn't work and we'd choose the other's path next time.

The truth is, there is no right way to share with those who have never had close experience with long-term illness. And for each new season you go through in your life, one of your friends may be going through their own tough season at the same time. They may be their happiest ever when you're at your worst, or going through their own divorce when you're battling to stay alive. When that happens, neither of you is the right person to support the other through that season.

Whatever groove you're trying to get out of, find a mentor further down the path, a group of humans who are currently walking the journey a few steps ahead or behind, and be open to a friend that God will give you to support your latest endeavour—a friend for a reason, a season, or a lifetime.

The Accountability Partner

Lastly, if you're proactively trying to change your life, get an accountability partner. And pay money that hurts your back pocket for them.

I've come to realise that any change that's ever stuck in my life is when I've paid heavily for an accountability partner. There will *never* be enough time or willpower to change long-term grooves in the road when it comes to a step-change, next-level impact.

When I decided to write this book, I truly could not find a moment in my day. Running three businesses, managing clients' money, keeping on top of the global markets, building new courses, producing a weekly podcast, and being a mum to three children (all with different schedules) meant there honestly was no time.

But, like Stephen Covey showed in his seminal work, *The Seven Habits of Highly Effective People*, I've come to know that it all can be done with enough desire and priority. And nothing focuses the mind like investing money that hurts in your success.

So I hunted down a human who is phenomenally talented at looking inside the craziness of the mind, with a totally different approach than anything I'd ever read or heard about, and handed over a fortune of dollars—at least, a fortune when you're earning in South African Rands. That level of investment means that I *never* miss a weekly session, I do all my homework for each week, and I wrote the first draft of my book in twenty-seven days.

Paying for accountability changes the conversation in your head from whether or not you *feel* like doing something to whether or not you feel like wasting your hard-earned money. Not many of us do feel like wasting our hard-earned money, and we are determined to get a return on investment. So despite wanting to crawl into bed after a horrible day today, I'm writing. And I'm so grateful I'm doing it, and not making the two years of talking about it, three.

Another accountability tool I use is one of public accountability. Whenever I need to get something done and I'm struggling, I'll announce it on my podcast or social media and include a date for going live. I've used it every year to achieve my One Thing for that year. The fear of not achieving that goal, of failure, and of public shame, gets me to deliver—and my tribe holds me accountable for it by asking how I'm progressing.

I don't think any of us are strong enough to make the big, structural changes we all need to in order to live our best lives, alone. Well, maybe I'm not as capable as you are, but I know for sure that I have achieved what I have, and that I am where I am today, *because* of the tools I've used, and the people I've drawn alongside me on this journey. They just add that extra bit of sparkle and energy to an otherwise difficult task.

The pull of The World Out There is strong because you change the status quo of your relationships with those around and threaten their own sense of security in their groove. Those grooves are deep, and it's so easy to get sucked back in—ask anyone who has ever tried to stay sober or clean from drugs. If you want to make any change, you need to get a great mentor, a support group of people in a similar situation, a friend who understands what you're going through, and—if it's change you're proactively making—an accountability partner you pay wallet-burning amounts to make sure you achieve your goal!

JOURNALING

For the changes you need to make to achieve your vision,

- Who can you follow to inspire and teach you how to make the change? Get their book, listen to their podcast, watch their videos, join their groups.

- Which people or groups of people do you need to be more careful with in sharing the details of your new groove?
- Who can you pay to provide the accountability and knowledge you need to get your change sorted? Find out what's available from there, and what it costs. When debating cost, you may need to go back to your why not (what will it cost you to *not* achieve this change) and weigh that against what it is you're doing.

If you're wanting to join an amazingly supportive group who will cheer you on for any change you want to make—in the health, wealth, work, relationship, or mindset shifts you need to live your Best Life—join our Facebook group, Deep Grooves with Lisa Linfield, www.facebook.com/groups/BraveToBeFree.

18

Getting Stuff Done:
The Practices That Nurture
Your Best Life Tree

We all tend to overestimate what we can do in the short term and underestimate what we can achieve in the long term. I know that when I think about my businesses, I get frustrated, because I feel that for the amount of work I do I should be a whole lot further down the road. But then when I look back, I'm actually amazed at how much I have done.

The biggest challenge about any change is that the results lag behind the work. Fixing a relationship? You've got to consistently work hard for the other person to start trusting again and then only after a while will they start responding. Trying to build a business? Oh wow, now there's a lag between work done and results achieved. Trying to instil long term fitness? Goodness, that takes a whole bunch of work before one person will notice.

But the biggest thing I can tell you is consistency wins every time. Showing up, doing the stuff, every single day. Get rich quick, crash diets, and bursts of effort in a relationship never ever resulted in long term sustainable change. Lotto winners lose the cash, the weight gets put back on (and then some), and you erode trust with yourself. You have a 1 in 4,000 chance of getting rich quickly, but a 3 in 100 chance of doing it the by hard work. So you're 120 times more likely to become a dollar millionaire the old fashioned way.

I'm a voracious reader of nonfiction books that will help me succeed at living my Best Life, so I thought I'd summarise a few of my best productivity hacks I've gathered for you to get out of the grooves that are holding you back.

1. Rhythms

One of the best skills I learnt in my time as an executive of a retail banking distribution channel team was a mantra called Structure, Rigor, Discipline. When you're trying to get thousands of people to walk in the same direction, you can't just wing it. In HBDI, those great talents lie in the thinking style which is not one of my natural strengths. But I was grateful to spend six years in that environment to stretch my abilities and learn the tools I needed for success.

Rhythms are daily, weekly, monthly, quarterly, and annual routines you put in place to make sure you deliver on your goals. They're personal and organisational non-negotiables that you just do. No debate. You can download a summary of them at www.LisaLinfield .com/DeepGroovesDownload.

Work-Life 18-Month Planning—2 Days

Every July, I do my big Goal Setting and Life Review. I find December or January too hectic—the family holidays, the end of year scramble from a work and children's perspective, and the southern hemisphere double whammy of having our major summer holiday all at once.

- I always begin with **reflection** (which takes around three hours) and have a standard process I take myself through. It starts with looking at the personal and professional achievements (the leaves and fruits of my tree) and an evaluation of my branches of effort and my Support Six of the tree trunk (the inner core of Thinking, Health, Wealth, Work, Happiness, and the bark of Wisdom). Then I focus on lessons learnt and, lastly, gratitude.
- Then I **look forward**. I spend some time dreaming, visioning, revisiting my whys and why nots, going through my values,

and coming up with my five-year goals for each of my Support Six. I always have a primary focus area for the year. Last year it was work—getting my company up and running—and this year it's health.

- Then I turn to the **One Thing** in each of the Support Six that I need to achieve this year and figure out the key milestones through the year that need to happen to meet that goal. I get it down to a clear, concise goal for each of the Support Six that I know is a stretch but possible, that I believe I can own, and I know I can find a pathway to making it happen.

- **Planning**. Work and life for me are very integrated, so the next level of planning always involves looking first at our family calendar and then planning my goals and work around that to make sure that when we go on vacation, I'm able to switch off completely.

- Next, I focus on the **Thinking Stacks** I'll need to nail to get myself to the next level. I do Reverse Thinking Stacks for any goals I know deep in my soul that I'm going to struggle to achieve, and work out the Good Reasons, Real Reasons and identity statements I'm telling myself.

- I then do my **Everyday Shortcuts to Power**, working out what affirmations, identity statements, liberating assumptions, and Suitcase Pictures I need to have to ensure I can meet my clear and concise goal.

Annual Checkup—1 Day

Each year between Christmas and New Year, I'll take a day to do a checkup on my goals and my Best Life Tree. It's a mini version of my Work-Life 18-Month Plan. I reflect on the past six months, revisit the goals if needed, and extend my plan by another six months so there's always a rolling eighteen-month plan.

Quarterly Checkup—Half Day

Once a quarter I do a mini checkup on and reforecasting of the quarter's goals. I don't update the plan; I just reconnect and plan for the quarter.

Monthly Planning—CEO Day (work)

Every month I take a full day that I call my CEO Day. It's the day I spend time with my CEO (God) to give thanks and plan and it is the most non-negotiable part of my month. I always start with a huge, yummy breakfast, where I take my journal and write my gratitude for the month that's been.

Then I call to mind my clients I've worked with and big projects I've worked through that month and the month to come, and I go through an action thinking cycle for each (see chapter two). I think about what happened, reflect on the experiences, see what I can learn, conclude what I need to do differently, and add relevant actions to my to-do list. Then I pray for my clients and projects.

After lunch, I focus on the month, doing Time Blocking. Time Blocking is when I go through my calendar and first fill in the big rocks—things that have to get done, like weekends away, all-day meetings, and client reviews and goals I need to achieve. Then I schedule a block of time to work on each of the major tasks at hand. It means that if during the month I have to move that item, it's a conscious decision to de-prioritise it.

Lastly, I focus on my numbers. Your business finances are the lifeblood of your work success, and it's one of those things you just have to do. As I teach people in my free 6 Day Sprint (www.6daysprint.com), the average person spends one hour a month on finances. But when you dig deeper, over 90 percent spend no time on it. How will you be fit if you spend no time exercising? How will you do well at work if you never put in an the hours or improve your skills? You won't. So if you want your personal finances or your business finances to do well, you need to spend time on it.

Weekly Planning

Each week I do weekly planning. I adjust my calendar time blocks, work out priorities, and make sure I'm not dropping the ball. I also update my finances.

Daily Practices

Goodness, I would love to tell you I'm a superwhizz at the dailies. This is my hardest area because it involves my lifelong battle between my duvet and my alarm clock. When I'm at my best, I'll wake up at 5:00 a.m. or 5:30 a.m. (depending on the school lifts and gym schedule), and do twenty minutes of gym, twenty minutes of prayer / meditation / Bible-reading, and twenty minutes of journaling and planning. You should know by now, my journaling is NEVER "Dear diary, This is what happened to me yesterday . . ." It's Reverse Thinking Stack journaling trying to work out why my day before went pear-shaped, dreams and goals journaling, affirmation journaling, etc.

At my worst, I just do my twenty minutes of Bible-reading and prayer, since that truly is the water to my roots. I use a daily reading study guide, which forces me to think of topics totally different to my daily grind and opens up my Reticular Activating System to scan my life and thinking on that topic. This morning, for example, my reading was on the unique gifts each one of us has and how important it is to use it for our purpose of serving others. So through the day my brain scanned for opportunities to serve others.

Then I always have my 'Bare Minimums' of an hour of personal training twice a week. So no matter how off the rails I go, my health block has a Bare Minimum of two hours of hard training. Bare Minimums are crucial to ensuring you never go totally off the rails. In health I have a Bare Minimum of never eating wheat—as I'm so intolerant—which means I just never go there on bread, pasta, cakes etc.

One thing I do is use a tracker in my journal to note how many times I'm doing each of these morning routines a week. I aim for a minimum of four times per week for each of them. Over seven days, it works out that I hit that most of the time. What it does help me with is my I *am* statements. If I'm planning more than 50 percent of the week, then I can say I *am* a planner. Now that goes against every fibre in my previous identity because I'm not one of those planning, organised types. So it's helping me re-shift my identity. I *am* an early riser. Wow. Now there's something I never thought I'd say!

My final daily practice is that I always keep Sundays free as a family day. I never work. It truly is the best discipline I've ever introduced. Even if I work till midnight on Saturday, I don't work on Sundays. My family is way more understanding of Saturday work if they know they have my full attention on Sunday. My brain also gets one day to totally switch off, since I never think, "I should be working." It's my Sabbath—I honour God—and so it's a no-go zone. If there is a weekend seminar, I make sure the following weekend I don't work on the Saturday and have the whole weekend with my girls, and I'll usually take the Monday off as well.

2. One Thing and Habits

I mentioned earlier in this chapter that I choose One Thing each year that I think will be pivotal in enabling me to achieve many other things—both as a theme, and then for each of my Support Six. If you want to get things done, you need to be selective about what you focus on. This idea comes from Gary Keller's book *The One Thing* that shows when you have only one thing to focus on, you are more likely to get it done. When you have a list of two, three, or four things, your chances of getting them done drops off a cliff.

I love this quote from Gary:

> *"In any discussion about success, the words 'discipline' and 'habit' ultimately intersect. Though separate in meaning, they powerfully connect to form the foundation for achievement— **regularly working at something until it regularly works for you.** When you discipline yourself, you're essentially training yourself to act in a specific way. Stay with that long enough and it becomes routine—in other words, a habit. So when you see people who look*

*like 'disciplined' people, what you're really seeing is people who've trained a handful of habits into their lives. This makes them seem 'disciplined' when actually they're not. **No one is.**"* [1]

The only time you need discipline is in the sixty-six days you need to instil a habit. Once something has become a habit, it requires far less discipline. It's just the way things are, something you do each day.

Gary goes on to say,

> *"The trick is to choose the right habit and bring just enough discipline to establish it. . . . Don't be a disciplined person. Be a person of powerful habits and use selected discipline to develop them. Build one habit at a time. Success is sequential, not simultaneous. No one actually has the discipline to acquire more than one powerful new habit at a time. Super successful people aren't superhuman at all; they've just used selected discipline to develop a few significant habits. One at a time. Over time."* [2]

What is the one thing, the one habit you need to instil, that when you do, it will transform all the others. Charles Duhig calls these key-stone habits. That one thing unlocks all the others in that area. When it comes to health for example, the habit I'm working on is getting up when the alarm clock goes. If I can do that, I'll exercise. If I exercise, everything else stays on track.

When it comes to work, it may be a habit or it may be a project or focus area. My one focus area is getting myself out there, which I'm instilling in a habit—one hour on a Monday devoted to approaching people to be on podcasts, write a guest article, be on radio.

3. Be Organised

Whether it's instilling your *one* new habit or focusing on your One Thing, you will need some time in your week to do it. It comes down to prioritising your time and asking yourself how badly you want it.

The more organised you are, the more likely it is you will achieve your goal—something I've had to learn, because it doesn't come easily.

If you plan your week in advance and work out that the only time to do something is in the evening, then get a babysitter to look after the kids and go and do it. When you're paying someone for the two hours, it will hold you accountable to actually go and do what you need to do—exercise, work on your side hustle, go on a date night. A bit like my trainer, if you cancel too late, you'll need to pay, so you make sure you're ready and use that time to your best ability.

My weekly planning will often result in me arranging with John or my mum to pick up some of the home stuff so I can focus on squishing everything in. You need a team, and you need to ask. People aren't psychic.

If you're trying to stick to a health plan, being organised with your week's food and carving out time to prepare it is key to being able to stick to it. If you're not organised, when your blood sugar hits a low, you'll eat whatever's available, especially the chocolate. If you made sure there were healthy snacks made on Sunday night, you'd reach for one of them, increasing your chance for success.

When I look back on my own challenges of eating healthily and not giving in to sugar, it's often because I don't have viable alternatives that can give me energy without having those sugar rushes, things like date balls or fat bombs.

It's the same with wealth. When people aren't organized with their money, they will spend more. I see it with kid's party gifts. If I haven't been organized and bought the presents early, I'll have to rush out and buy them. Because we're due at that party in five minutes' time, I'll reach for a present that's probably way too expensive but ticks the box.

Research shows that the people who are more able to stick to either money or eating plans are people who are organised and track it. They get a sense of accomplishment every single day with their little successes, which then motivates them to stick to it further.

I once asked a woman how she found the time to start her side hustle. She said she'd take her lunch hour away from everybody, sit with her computer, and work on her side hustle. I remember thinking to myself, who takes lunch hour breaks? But it then made me really think about protecting time slots to achieve your goals, and your lunch hour is yours to take and use. It just comes down to the question, "How badly do you want it?" Time is there; you just need to prioritise it.

4. The Very Next Step

I learned this particular technique from David Allen's book *Getting Things Done*. If you want to achieve your goal, you need to focus on the very next step you need to take. Not the big goal; literally the very next step.

If your goal for the week is to register a business, don't put "register a business" on your to-do list. Write the very next step, which might be "phone Mary and ask her who she used to register her business." Then, once you know that, cross it off. The next thing you put on your to-do list would be "email Mary's recommendation about kicking off the process to register a business." And then cross that off the list once that's done.

The challenge with the "register a business" goal is that it may feel overwhelming. "Lose a kilogram this week" is one of those too. Break it down into the very next step you need to take that day and focus on that, always ensuring that that goal is aligned to your One Thing.

5. Pre-Visioning: When the Going Gets Tough

Understand that things will go pear-shaped. You will slip back into your old grooves and habits, and you will have days when you're unable to be the human you want to be for so many reasons. The secret is to get back on that path as quickly as possible. This is one of my really difficult things when it comes to my health!

This is when you need to rely on two tools: I can do hard things and pre-visioning.

As I mentioned in chapter five, I can do hard things is a mantra I repeat to myself, often through gritted teeth.

Each of us has done very hard things in our lives. In my "16 Week Side Hustle" course, one of the examples I give that always makes people stop and think is the concept of overtime working. At some stage, all of us have worked late nights and weekends for a corporate employer—having the discipline to sacrifice personal time, despite how tired we are, to further someone else's profit objectives. So why don't we dig deep and do it for ourselves to further our own goals, to have the freedom that comes with earning more money and building a business we love?

Whatever it is you're trying to achieve, you've done harder things before. You can do this too. I know you can. Now, at a calm time, find an example in your life of something in a similar vein that was hard, so when the trouble hits the fan and you want to give up, you can draw on it as a Memory Photograph and say, "I can do hard things!"

That exercise is called pre-visioning. In a time of calmness when you're motivated to achieve your goals, you imagine something with so much feeling and strength that you can use it to overcome something difficult. Every Olympian has a pre-visioning sequence they go through the night before and the day of their race—and it helps them get through nerves of the event. They imagine the habits they'll need and implement those habits when times get tough.

The Habit Model

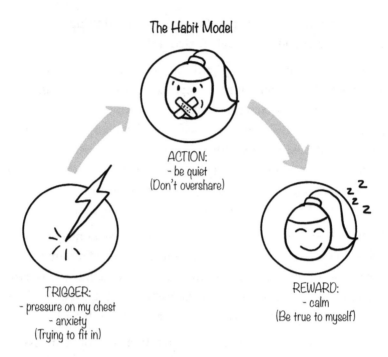

ACTION:
- be quiet
(Don't overshare)

TRIGGER:
- pressure on my chest
- anxiety
(Trying to fit in)

REWARD:
- calm
(Be true to myself)

It comes down to Charles Duhig's work on habits I mentioned in chapter six. Pre-vision the triggers that may set you off course, plan the course of action you will take, and be clear on the reward.

Remember when I discovered I was trying too hard for the network lunch by searching through my power dresses? When I became aware that I was trying to fit in rather than belong again, I decided beforehand on my action plan for the lunch later that day. The trigger was the feeling of anxiety, the elephant sitting on my chest. I pre-visioned that my action would be to stay quiet—shut the flock up—and I knew that my reward would be a sense of calm (and not the frenzied panic of worrying if I'd overshared or said the right thing).

Another example was working on my side hustle. My trigger was putting my babies to bed after family supper; my routine was go to the TV room and switch on a mindless show; then the reward was brain numbing. When I uncovered this routine, I made sure that once I'd put my babies to bed, I didn't even turn right to the TV room—I made myself turn left and head straight to my study. It worked amazingly well.

You can anticipate roadblocks—not getting up when your alarm goes off, chocolate at 8 p.m., watching TV at night instead of working on your side hustle. Whatever it is, pre-vision your behaviour as part of your morning routine, and then each time that trigger comes, it will be easier and easier to default to an action that serves you rather than causes you to stumble.

Whilst your Thinking is the core of your tree, the deep roots are what will determine whether your Best Life Tree will blossom or not. These practices are what will result in the tree blossoming, the beautiful fruits and leaves growing, and the happiness that results.

As Gary Keller said, build one habit at a time. Don't try land them all—just start out on the road.

JOURNALING

Prioritise which of these practices that nurture your Best Life Tree you will focus on. Choose one and detail your plan of action. Then commit at least sixty-six days to making it a habit.

19

Transitioning

Robin Sharma has a quote I love:

All change is hard at first, messy in the middle
and so gorgeous in the end.[1]

There truly is no two ways about it. The space shuttle burns most of its fuel just leaving the earth's surface and fighting the force of gravity and very little to go the hundreds of kilometres to the moon and back. That's how change works—it takes effort to fight the force to return to the safety and security of your familiar groove of behaviour, groove of relationship, groove of unhealthy living, groove of unfulfilling work. Living permanently in a new way will require you to focus so single-mindedly on achieving your goal that other things *will* get dropped—not may, will.

These last five years of my life have seen me earn an honours degree, go through my board certification, leave corporate and start two online businesses, launch a podcast that's been listened to in over a hundred countries, launch and relaunch four online courses, speak on many stages, and build a profitable face-to-face wealth management business. I've written this book; been featured on radio, in international sites (such as Forbes and Arianna Huffington's Thrive Global), and on other people's podcasts; and taught a whole bunch of home helpers, school kids and first jobbers about money as my give-back.

Have I dropped balls? Many. Oh, my goodness, many. Just today my husband and I sat giggling on a school bench as I'd somehow got our date wrong for the twins' parent-teacher conference, and we were the only people in a dead school. I have spent far too little time with my friends in the last five years, and my soul misses them. Our weekends at our river house used to be filled with friends but are now spent with just the five of us, as I work every Saturday. And I'm definitely not in peak health and am over my normal weight.

But when I rate myself for my Support Six, I know that I have managed to score myself at least eight out of ten on most of the important stuff—my Thinking and mental health; my Happiness in my immediate family; Wealth and Work; and my Wisdom or spiritual health).

I've learnt in life to preface everything with "for now," since it all changes in a moment. But for now, I'm closer to God than I've been in ages as I cling for dear life as we roller-coaster through this amazing adventure. For now, John and I are just so grateful that we ended up being able to walk this journey in life, and I think I am the luckiest girl in the world to have him as my husband. For now, each day I get to spend with my girls is a miracle—and I find it amazing that I was lucky enough to be their mum. And for now, my relationship with my parents and brother feeds my soul. For now, I'm grateful for work that fulfils me and wealth that sustains us. The only area in the primaries truly falling short is my health—more specifically, staying away from sugar.

But I miss my friends deeply. I am not good about rest time, things that bring me joy outside of work, play time. And I would love to be more involved in a community that gives back. Something's got to give, and these are the things in my life that have.

As tough as these five years have been, it's been the most deeply rewarding personal change journey.

When I started out trying to squish in a university honours degree, leave the corporate world, and start a business, I naturally believed that the biggest struggle would be the juggling—the time management, the lack of sleep, the exhaustion at times. Trying to live up to everyone's expectations and my own high standards.

What I never even considered was how much I'd need to learn and grow as a human—and how rewarding that would be. I had no idea how hard it would be, leaving the safety of the Deep Grooves of corporate, everything I ever knew and mastered, the safety of a hierarchy. How much I'd miss the praise from my bosses and colleagues, the joy of leading a team, despite being so ready to start my business and work on my dream. It was hard trying to find my identity and my self-esteem from within me and not the mirrors on the faces around me.

But the hardest journey of all has been the battle of my fears. Like all addicts, I will always be a recovering overachieving good little girl, struggling to find my sense of self and purpose in me and my true journey through life with God and not from the praise of others. But that only comes when you are prepared to be brave and go to battle with your fears.

The princess warrior is *never* brave sitting on the couch, eating popcorn, watching Netflix.

She is only brave in the face of fear. That fear is not usually in mid-battle—that's when the adrenaline kicks in—but the fear shows its ugliest face in those first steps toward battle when you could back out. That calm before the storm when every single fear rises from your darkest soul to give you every reason why you have no place stepping into the arena in the first place.

Imposter syndrome. Fear of failure. Vulnerability. The fear of your heart being trampled over. Fear of embarrassing yourself. The list goes on, as does the verbal abuse of Cruella in your head.

You must be brave—taking those steps of courage *despite* the fear—in order to be free. Don't give in to an out-of-date reptilian brain that wants to keep you safe, keep you in the tribe, keep you in the groove of The World Out There. Don't give in permanently to safe and secure, to maintaining the harmony and stability that keeps you from living your Best Life.

Every day, the way you think determines your actions. The thoughts you have are rooted in the Thinking Stacks you've developed over time. That thinking becomes the central core in the actions of your life—and will either bear fruit and luscious leaves or result in bare branches and a bleak garden.

It's therefore our job to understand our brain, to step outside our lives and be mindful of every action and every word that points to our deep Thinking Stacks. We must do the work to excavate away until we leave the realm of Good Reasons, lazy thinking, and faulty assumptions, and we embrace the Ah-Ha moments that come with uncovering the Real Reasons for our thinking, the Real Reasons for our behaviour.

Only then will we be able to consciously choose a path of new behaviour, new habits, new goals, and new dreams. We may choose the same path we're currently on, in the groove we've been in all our life, with a few small tweaks—but at least we choose it consciously and not by default because it's always been done that way.

But we may discover a different path to a different life. A path that we sense exists, that uses our unique gifts, our passions for a greater purpose. A path that stretches us, builds deep strong roots of thinking that allow our lives to blossom and produce happiness, bone-deep joy, and an energy that never runs out.

It is hard to change paths, to walk through unchartered territory. But you never need to go through it completely alone. There will always be people out there to walk with you on your journey. They may not look like the fairy tales tell you they will. But they're out there—for a season, a reason, or a lifetime. Find them, stay close to them, and appreciate the gift of them. Each one is God's gift, His hands on earth, His love in human form.

Go on, pick up your journal, and take these first steps. They are the hardest, but the rewards are greater than you'll ever imagine.

Call to Action

If you enjoyed this book and want to put into practice all you've learnt through a guided process, please visit www.LisaLinfield.com and sign up for the companion course to the book. In it, I take you through the book in a deeper, visual, more interactive way, accompanied by a beautiful workbook of exercises and reflections that will help you to take your journey further toward your Best Life.

You were created to live an amazing life, not just survive it.

You just need to do the thinking work to achieve it!

Notes

Introduction

1. John A. Shedd, as quoted in Fred R. Shapiro, *The Yale Book of Quotations* (Yale University Press: New Haven, 2006), 705.
2. Peter Densen, MD, "Challenges and Opportunities Facing Medical Education," *Transactions of the American Clinical and Climatological Association* 122 (2011): 48–58, https://www.ncbi.nlm.nih.gov/pmc/articles/PMC3116346/.
3. Nancy Kline, *More Time to Think: The power of independent thinking* (Octopus Publishing Group Ltd, 2015):15.

2: Removing the Weeds That Strangle Our Best Life Tree

1. Dr. Abby Medcalf, "Talking to your partner about money with Dr Abby Medcalf," *Working Women's Wealth Podcast.* 2019. https://workingwomenswealth.com/86
2. Brené Brown, *Dare to Lead* (Random House, 2018), 147–148. I recommend you download the core list of emotions from https://brenebrown.com/downloads
3. Rachel Grate, "Science Shows Something Surprising about People Who Still Journal," Mic.com, Feb. 17, 2015. https://www.mic.com/articles/110662/science-shows-something-surprising-about-people-who-still-journal#.n0QO5ApTN.
4. Karen A. Baikie and Kay Wilhelm, "Emotional and Physical Health Benefits of Expressive Writing," *Advances in Psychiatric Treatment* 11, no.5 (September 2005): 338–46. https://doi.org/10.1192/apt.11.5.338
5. J.W. Pennebaker and S.K. Beall, "Confronting a Traumatic Event: Toward an Understanding of Inhibition and Disease," *Journal of Abnormal Psychology* 95, no. 3 (August 1986): 274–81. https://www.ncbi.nlm.nih.gov/pubmed/3745650.
6. As referenced in Sam McLeod, "Kolb's Learning Styles and Experimental Learning Cycle," SimplyPsychology.com, 2017. https://www.simplypsychology.org/learning-kolb.html.

5: Assumptions Become Our Identity

1. Brittany Hoopes, "Setting and achieving your goals with goal expert Brittany Hoopes," *Working Women's Wealth.* 2018. https://workingwomenswealth.com/35

6: Fitting In Versus Belonging

1. Brené Brown, *Braving the Wilderness* (Random House, 2017).

2. Brené Brown, *The Gifts of Imperfection* (Hazelden Publishing, 2010). Emphasis added.
3. This was first described by Martin M. Broadwell in February 1969 in his article "Teaching for Learning (XVI)" which can be seen at http://www.wordsfitlyspoken .org/gospel_guardian/v20/v20n41p1-3a.html. Gordon Training International popularised it.
4. Charles Duhigg, *The Power of Habit* (William Henemann, 2012).

7: The Groove

1. Danny Gokey, "Tell Your Heart to Beat Again," track 3 on *Hope in Front of Me*, BMG Records, 2014, compact disk. Emphasis mine.

8: The Gap

1. Marianne Williamson, *A Return to Love: Reflections on the Principles of a Course in Miracles* (Thorsons, 1996).

9: Listening to Your Guiding Signposts

1. Walid Azami on Azul Terronez, "Walid Azami: From Teacher Credential Dropout to Celebrity Photographer," *Authors Who Lead*. Podcast audio, 47:10, October 11, 2019. https://coachazul.com/blog/episode70/.
2. Lisa Linfield on Tammy Gooler Loeb, "Follow your gut, not just your skills," *Work from the Inside Out*, 2019.

10: Understanding the Signposts That Have Been

1. Margaret Hefferman, "Forget the Pecking Order at Work," TEDWomen 2015, https://www.ted.com/talks/margaret_heffernan_forget_the_pecking_order_at_ work.
2. Pat Flynn, *Will it Fly?* (Flynndustries, 2016).

11: Understanding the Signposts That Are Now

1. Susan Jeffers, *Feel the Fear and Do It Anyway* (Ballantine Books, 2006): Location 136 in Kindle.
2. Ibid., Location 225 in Kindle.
3. Brené Brown, *The Gifts of Imperfection* (Hazelden Publishing, 2010), 40. Emphasis added.
4. Ibid., 46.

12: Looking from the Outside In

1. Theodore Roosevelt, "Citizenship in a Republic" (speech, Paris, France, April 23, 1910), Leadership Now, https://www.leadershipnow.com/tr-citizenship.html.
2. Kesha, "This Is Me," track 7 on *The Greatest Showman: Reimagined*, Atlantic Records, 2017, compact disk.

13: Permission to Dream

1. See Edwin A. Locke, "Toward a Theory of Task Motivation and Incentives." *Organizational Behavior and Human Performance* 3, no. 2 (May 1968): 157–89.
2. C.R. Snyder, Kevin L. Rand and David R. Sigmon, "Hope Theory: A Member of the Positive Psychology Family." *The Oxford Handbook of Hope* (Oxford University Press, 2018): 257–258
3. Watershed, "Breathing," track 3 on *Staring At The Ceiling*, EMI Music, 2008, compact disk.
4. Jim Collins, *Built to Last*, (HarperCollins Publishers, 2011).
5. Nicholas Winton. Interview with Anderson Cooper. *60 Minutes*. CBS News. May 2014.
6. Gloria Mitchell, "Resilience: overcoming the impossible," *Working Women's Wealth Podcast*. 2019. https://workingwomenswealth.com/41

14: Free Your Mind for the Best Chance of Success

1. Nancy Kline, *More Time to Think: The Power of Independent Thinking* (Octopus, 2009): 38.

15: Rocket Fuel

1. Angela L. Duckworth, et al., "Cognitive and Noncognitive Predictors of Success," *Proceedings of the National Academy of Sciences* 116, no. 47 (November 2019): 23499–504.

18: Getting Stuff Done: The Practices That Nurture Your Best Life Tree

1. Gary Keller and Jay Papasan, *The ONE Thing: The Surprisingly Simple Truth Behind Extraordinary Results* (Bard Press, 2013): Location 556 in Kindle
2. Ibid., Location 562 in Kindle

19: Transitioning

1. Robin Sharma, Twitter post, April 8, 2014, 3:00 a.m, https://twitter.com /robinsharma/status/453472361421877248?lang=en.

About the Author

L isa Linfield's journey has not been ordinary. Brave—yes. Successful—yes. Straightforward—never. She was a practicing physical therapist before joining the banking world in both the UK and South Africa, but she's also studied Theology at Oxford University and Corporate Finance at London Business School just to tap into the thinking of the world's great minds.

Having always aspired to be the best, she set herself the goal of becoming the CEO of a large company. But events led her to question whose goal that really was, and whether there wasn't something more to life out there that she should be doing.

So, after a successful twenty-year corporate career, she stepped off the ladder to start three businesses whose goal is to change the lives of people through financial freedom. That work has crystallised one central belief—we all get stuck in Deep Grooves of the way things are because we were never taught how to change our lives for the better.

Lisa is a board Certified Financial Planner® and has set a goal to teach one million women about money through her podcast and blog, *Working Women's Wealth*, as well as online courses, books and keynote speaking.

Lisa lives in Johannesburg, South Africa, with her husband, John, and three daughters, Jess, Isi, and Emma.

CPSIA information can be obtained
at www.ICGtesting.com
Printed in the USA
LVHW010346260720
661545LV00013B/374